Around the Mersey Valley

by Jen Darling

with the

Mersey Valley Partnership

Alfresco Books

ISBN 1 873727 05 4

British Library Cataloguing in Publication Data. A catalogue record for this book is available from the British Library.

First published in July 1994 by *Alfresco Books*
7 Pineways, Appleton, Warrington, Cheshire, WA4 5EJ
Telephone: 0925 267503

Publisher's Note: While every effort has been made to ensure that the information given in this book is correct the Publishers do not accept responsibility for any inaccuracy.

Cover by Gordon Firth. Water Colour of Hough Bridge and Hillcliffe.
Photographs by John Cocks
Maps by David Potts
Line drawings by David Potts, Gill Bond and Glenys Rowlands

Typeset and design by Jen Darling of *Alfresco Books*
Proof reading by Valerie West

Produced by *Coveropen Ltd.*, Wigan. *Telephone:* 0942 821831

FOREWORD

The Countryside on your Doorstep

Take some time to escape from the noise and stress of everyday life. Enjoy fresh air, views and the sounds and scents of the countryside close to home. Whatever the season, these pleasures are available nearby, free of charge, on walks in woodlands and by hedgerows, through parks and open countryside, and along the canals and streams of North Cheshire - in the Mersey Valley. With Jen Darling's excellent guide you can get to know your local countryside, confident of finding your way.

The *Mersey Valley Partnership* cares for the environment and manages the countryside around Runcorn, Warrington and Widnes. One of our tasks is to make it easier to find and follow country footpaths, and our countryside management team and volunteers clear overgrown paths, repair stiles and bridges, and mark the routes where possible.

The Rangers often lead guided walks in the area and details of these and other outdoor events can be found at Ranger Centres or on *Outline*, our recorded information line - 0928 580475.

Wishing you many pleasant walks, and hoping you enjoy the richness of the local landscape.

David Potts
Visitor Services and Interpretive Officer
Mersey Valley Partnership

Mersey Valley Partnership is funded by Cheshire County Council, Halton Borough Council and Warrington Borough Council, and is supported by the Countryside Commission.

ACKNOWLEDGMENTS

I would like to thank the *Mersey Valley Partnership* for giving me the idea for this publication, for providing so much invaluable information for inclusion in it and for their continuous co-operation throughout the whole project.

I would also like to thank all those who have done the walks in my other books and have let me know of any difficulties that have arisen. The information is always checked and each print run updated. I look forward to any constructive comments concerning *Walks in North Cheshire*.

FINDING AND USING FOOTPATHS

This book may give you the confidence to explore other paths and discover routes of your own. Here are some hints to help you do this successfully.

* Buy a Pathfinder map.

* Look for public footpath signs where the path leaves the road.

* Follow the line of the path, looking for clues to confirm that you are on the right route.

* Wooden signs with a yellow arrow and a walker often point the way. Stiles can sometimes be seen ahead which is also a help.

* Well used paths are seen by a well worn route on the ground.

* Paths usually follow a field edge but sometimes cut across the middle.

CONTENTS

USING THE BOOK ...

Walks in North Cheshire contains 30 rambles of varying lengths, from two to seven miles. Each walk has detailed information, plus a sketchmap to help you find your way.

The walks are suitable for the lone walker, for groups, for families with children and/or dogs. As the steepest gradient is little more than gently undulating these walks should suit both old and young, fit and fragile.

The time taken to complete each walk will very much depend upon the people involved, but as a rough and generous guide allow an hour for every two to three miles.

Travelling instructions are given from the nearest town and suitable parking places suggested at the start of each walk. Bus and train times are not mentioned as these seem to change so frequently they may well be inaccurate before the book goes to press.

Points of interest are given at the end of each walk. Nearby places to visit are also mentioned, so that a walk may perhaps be combined with a trip to one of these.

bluebells and red campion

INTRODUCTION

The aim of *Walks in North Cheshire* is to encourage both locals and visitors to enjoy the region's countryside on foot. Field footpaths, woodland walkways and bridleways are used wherever possible, and roads avoided.

Below is a small attempt to encapsulate the many facets which make up the area's unique character. This varies from heavy industry, both past and present, to the stress-free space of open countryside, the rustic charm of unspoilt, rural villages, and the never-failing magic of waterways, both natural and man-made.

History

Bronze Age barrows at Winwick, the Roman road at Appleton, ancient crosses at Appleton Thorn and Lymm - all give us glimpses of our distant past. The ruins of the 11th century Halton Castle stand high above the River Mersey at Runcorn, while more recent landmarks are the water tower at Norton and Daresbury's controversial, concrete column. Religion has also played its part: Norton Priory was home to 24 Augustinian canons in the 12th century, and churches date from the 14th century St. Oswald's at Winwick, with its famous pig, to the 19th century St. Matthew's at Stretton, with its equally well known clock.

Industry

The scars of industry provide an interesting insight into our ancestors' employment. Quarrying for Cheshire's attractive red sandstone is evident on Runcorn Hill and Pex Hill; Spike Island was the birthplace of the Chemical Industry, and the massive cooling towers of Fiddler's Ferry Power Station dominate the Widnes skyline.

Coalmines north of Burtonwood stand deserted, Greenall's Wilderspool brewery is shut, but soap manufacture still continues at Warrington's Bank Quay. Here, the only railway transporter in the world can still be seen; other features from the Age of the Train are the skew bridge at Latchford and the huge, soot-smeared viaducts of Arley and Dutton.

Waterways

For centuries the **River Mersey** formed the natural boundary between Lancashire and Cheshire until, in the 1960s, the Labour government moved Widnes and Warrington into Cheshire in order to increase both the county's industry and its population.

The River Mersey is navigable for 19 miles from its estuary at Liverpool to Warrington. The steel suspension bridge that joins Widnes to Runcorn is an attractive sight. Completed in 1961 it was then the longest bridge of its kind in Europe and was built to replace an earlier transporter.

One walk drops down to the **River Weaver**, which is completely in Cheshire from its source near the hamlet of Peckforton, to its entry into the River Mersey near Frodsham. The River Weaver was made navigable in the 18th century, to carry salt from Nantwich, Winsford and Northwich, to Runcorn docks for export. All the locks along its course are manned by keepers but today road transport has creamed off much of its trade.

The **Manchester Ship Canal** roughly follows the course of the River Mersey. Almost 37 miles long with five locks, it was opened by Queen Victoria in 1894 when she sailed up its length from Liverpool to Manchester. It was directly responsible for making Manchester into one of Britain's largest seaports, despite being 32 miles from the coast. An enormous amount of industry has grown up along its banks and it has some of the largest swing bridges in the country.

Designed by the famous engineer, James Brindley, and opened in 1765, the **Bridgewater Canal** was the first English arterial canal. It extends for 28 miles from Worsley, near Manchester, to Runcorn, where it used to enter the River Mersey via a staircase of ten locks.

Although originally built to distribute coal from Worsley, it also had a variety of other uses: it transported raw cotton from Liverpool to the Manchester mills, and it operated a passenger service. Two of the stopping points for this were Stockton Heath and Lymm, and the fare was 1d per mile! Nowadays, the canal is used by pleasure craft and anglers, and several of these walks follow its towpath.

First bridging point on the River Mersey, this soaring span links Runcorn with Widnes.

Other canals which feature on several walks are the **Sankey Navigation** and the **Latchford to Runcorn Canal.**

Many interesting features can still be seen from the canal bank. Spare balance beams and stop planks (used when locks are drained for repairs) are to be found near locks. These are often protected from the weather by a roof, or are slotted into a special chamber under a bridge. The curved path, often made from brick with foot-stops for easy purchase, is another feature to be found at locks, and of course there's a lock-keeper's cottage, sometimes with a small-holding attached.

The Countryside

Rich farmland has always been found around the Mersey Valley. Cornfields and market gardening dominate the northern hinterland, while fields of barley for the brewing industry and rape for its oilseed colour the southern landscape.

A bonus reaped from the New Town's heyday has been a plethora of new parklands, expertly managed by the Ranger Services. These can be found throughout the region: from Pex Hill to Culcheth Linear Park, from Lymm Dam to Runcorn Hill. Each has its own inimitable character and topography, plus an immense diversity of fauna and flora and many meandering footpaths.

Mersey Forest is a new community forest stretching north-south from Sefton to Delamere and east-west from Ellesmere Port to Warrington.

People and Places

Pretty, unspoilt villages sprinkle the area; there's cobbled Grappenhall, the lighthouse at Hale and the Seneschal's house at Halton. Other buildings have also stood the test of time: the 14th century tithe barn at Arley, 15th century Bewsey Old Hall and Speke's Elizabethan manor house. And for a literary slant, the early life of Lewis Carroll comes into vivid focus on the Daresbury and Hatton walks.

Long Distance Routes

The **Trans-Pennine Trail**, stretching coast-to coast from Southport to Hull, is gradually being completed. It consists of a footpath, bridleway and cycleway route, sometimes running as three separate trails and at others 'braided'. In North Cheshire it follows sections of the *Mersey Way*.

Some of the walks in this book use part of the **Mersey Way** - a network of routes following the River Mersey, and other waterways such as the St. Helens Canal, the Black Bear Canal and the New Cut. Places along the route include: Hale, Spike Island, Fiddlers Ferry, Howley, Kingsway Bridge and the Woolston New Cut.

Howley suspension bridge

The Way covers almost twenty miles of North Cheshire around Widnes and Warrington, and there are numerous access points. It offers people somewhere to walk close to these built-up areas but in peace and quiet, where there are waterside views, historical interest and wildlife.

A Walker's Code
You may wander the paths of our fair countryside
But please use the stiles, don't leave gates open wide.
Follow the waymarks on routes we have planned,
With dogs in control and your kids close at hand.
Please don't damage the plants, take your litter back home,
Have a care for the wildlife wherever you roam.

The idyllic Bridgewater Canal runs through the heart of North Cheshire.

EQUIPMENT

Very little equipment is needed to tackle the walks in this book and it is best to travel as light as possible. However, here are one or two tips.

Maps In the introduction to each section details of the relevant Ordnance Survey Map are given. In each case the map used is one of the Pathfinder Series of Great Britain (1:25000). These are ideal for walkers as they give so much detail, even down to field boundaries. Ideally, one should invest in the appropriate one before starting out. A map reference is also given for the starting point of each walk.

Although the instructions have been made as clear as possible, occasionally the route is altered, signs get moved or new roads are built; also, what might seem clear to one person isn't necessarily so to another - or you might have been chatting ...! So do use your common sense and bear in mind that the author is not infallible either!

Footwear Although boots are normally the ideal footwear for a walker, in wet weather wellingtons are better for crossing muddy or cow-mired fields and, during a dry Summer, trainers are perfectly adequate. (Nylon socks cause blisters so stick to cotton or wool.)

Waterproofs Take an anorak or cagoule to cope with the vagaries of the British climate, plus a pair of over-trousers if you have them.

Sweaters It is better to start off warm and then shed clothes. Two layers are warmer than one thick layer. One of the nice things about taking up walking as a hobby, or just for pleasure occasionally, is that nobody cares what you look like. If you get hot, sling a sweater round your waist. In cold weather make sure you have hat, scarf, gloves, warm socks and waterproof footwear; it's miserable to have cold extremities!

Money A small amount of loose change is handy in case you need to make a 'phone call, stock up on chocolate bars, or spot a likely place for liquid refreshment!

Miscellaneous Carry as little as possible but a lightweight rucksack is useful for oddments like plasters and food. A hot drink in a thermos is also very acceptable on a cold day.

Wherever you go follow ...

THE COUNTRY CODE

Enjoy the countryside but respect its life and work.
Leave livestock, crops and machinery alone.
Keep dogs under close control.
Take special care on country roads.
Keep to public paths across farmland.
Use gates and stiles to cross fences, hedges and walls.
Fasten all gates.
Protect all wild life, plants and trees.
Help to keep all water clean.
Guard against all risk of fire.
Make no unnecessary noise.
Take **all** your litter home.

All the walks in this book are on public rights of way or alternatives agreed with the landowner. It is your right to use these paths but please remember that they cross land which is owned by another person. Please do not stray from the paths and respect private property.

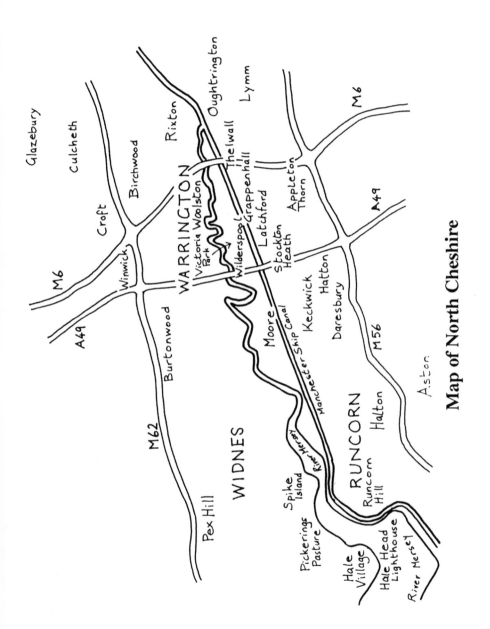

Map of North Cheshire

lapwing

partridge

skylark

NORTH EAST OF WARRINGTON

Birchwood	Glazebury
Croft	Rixton
Culcheth	Woolston

Map
The relevant Pathfinder maps are: Eccles (SJ 69/79) for all the above walks except Woolston, which is found on Warrington (SJ 68/78).

Farmland
The area to the north, around Culcheth, Croft and Glazebury, is fairly level farmland with wide easterly views to the gritstone Pennines. Two types of contrasting soil types are found here - both the result of the Ice Age. Melting ice covered all the underlying rock with clay - leading to a mineral-rich soil. This has probably been used for growing corn since it was cleared of forest by the Saxons.

Ground-nesting birds are a feature of the open countryside here, with lapwings present all year. In Winter large flocks form which, in Spring, become very noisy as they set up territories and guard nests. Another welcome sign of Spring is the skylarks' soaring song. Partridges also feed and breed in the cornfields and meadows, and may provide unwary walkers with a stunning surprise if they explode from nearby vegetation.

In the south of the area, some of the larger hollows in the clay became large lakes which gradually silted up and turned into peat bogs, dominated by the spongy plant, sphagnum. The best known of these are Chat Moss and Risley Moss. In other places too, low-lying, boggy land is flooded in wet weather by streams flowing down to the River Mersey. In fact, much of this area was impassable and dangerous until reclaimed about a hundred years ago by drainage, then fertilised by marl dug from pits on the edge of the mosses. In these areas the local clay sub-soil has produced high-grade farmland and the rich, peaty earth has proved most productive for market gardening.

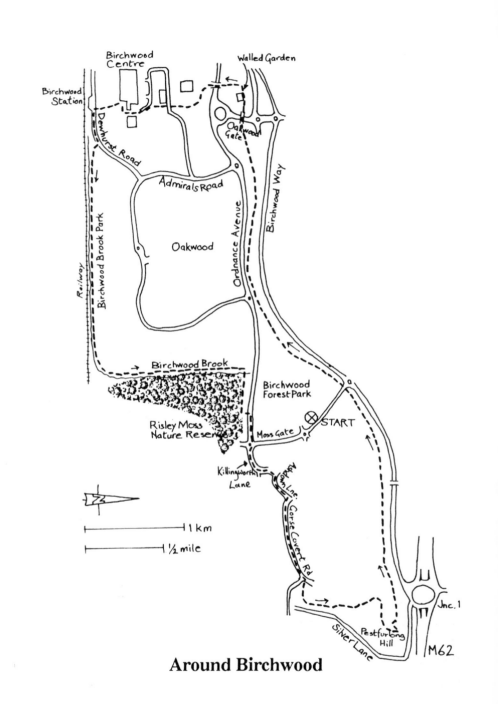

Around Birchwood

AROUND BIRCHWOOD

Distance: 6 miles

Start: Moss Gate (SJ 663 923)

By Car: From Warrington, take the A574 (Birchwood Way). Cross over the M6 and turn right down Moss Gate, where a screened car park is on the right.

Turn left out of the car park, then left again up steps at the roundabout. Take the right fork and keep right, parallel to the main road (Birchwood Way), until you reach a footbridge over Oakwood Gate. Cross this and turn first left. At the T-junction by the Walled Garden (which is worth a visit) turn left again.

Keep straight on over the footbridge and continue left on the main track. Then take the right fork towards the Birchwood Centre. Go past Spectrum Arena, then turn right and left past the Silver Birch pub towards the station. Cross Dewhurst Road and turn left.

After 200 yards turn right into Birchwood Brook Park. Now follow Birchwood Brook, keeping to the right for nearly a mile. Turn right at the T-junction near Ordnance Avenue, then take a left fork and follow the main path to Ordnance Avenue, which you cross and turn right.

Over the roundabout follow Killingworth Lane, turning right into Ashdown Lane. Turn right into Gorse Covert Road and pass four closes on the right. Straight after Rockingham Close turn onto the cinder path. After 100 yards turn left and follow the path to a gate. Here, turn right following the bridle path to Pestfurlong Hill.

From the hilltop turn left to join the path towards Birchwood. Keep straight on parallel to Birchwood Way (ignoring paths to the left). Drop down steps near the roundabout at Moss Gate and turn left back to your starting point.

silver birch

Birchwood's History

Before the 2nd World War a peaceful, rural community comprising 30 tenant farms surrounded the old village of Risley, the land having been laboriously reclaimed from peat bog for arable farming. However, with the onset of war, a Royal Ordnance Factory was built, which covered many acres of farmland between Woolston and Risley. Its lonely site, in a hollow often shrouded in mist, and its accessibility for the workforce from Liverpool and Manchester, made it an ideal location.

During the War about 30,000 people were employed there, many of them women, and over a million bombs, mines and shells were produced. It was vital but dangerous work and, to relieve the tension, everyone listened to *Workers Playtime* on the wireless in the canteen.

The factory was closed in 1945 although it acted as the Navy's rum store until 1961! In 1956 the United Kingdom Atomic Energy Authority (UKAEA) built its northern headquarters on part of the site, keeping sheds once used for shell-filling as storage depots.

However, despite this, the area became one of the largest derelict sites in Europe - until Warrington's development as a New Town transformed it into today's Birchwood, a fine example of how living landscapes can improve the quality of an urban environment. (Surprisingly, the armaments factory took twice as long to demolish as it did to build.)

Relics from the Past

The mounds on the playing fields hide four impregnable bunkers of reinforced concrete, where explosives were stored. In the 1980s, these bunkers provided valuable storage space for various local organisations and one housed a fascinating display of the area's history. Sadly, the Borough Council have now filled them with ash from Fiddler's Ferry Power Station.

Situated along the old Warrington-Leigh road, **Oakwood Gate** was one of the factory's three main entrances where a bus service stopped. It was also the site of an administration block, laundry and small hostel. **Ordnance Avenue** follows the line of Avenue D, the main east-west road to the factory.

The **Walled Garden**, now planted with exotic plants, was once a reservoir providing water for the factory. On the south wall can be seen the wheel which once operated the sluice gate mechanism.

The modern **Birchwood Station** stands on the site of *Risley Halt*, which ferried both workers and materials to the factory. A few old wooden posts mark the site of its platform and old railway sleepers and fencing posts can still be seen - relics from the internal railway which ferried goods around the works.

The recently developed *Birchwood* probably derives its name from birch trees which once covered much of the Pestfurlong area. **Pestfurlong Hill** itself, which forms the park's backbone, grew out of the factory's rubble, and from its summit views extend as far as the Pennines and Wales. Today, its slopes are planted with native species, such as alder, oak and ash, and there are secluded ponds and mosses rich in wildlife.

A PLACE TO VISIT

Risley Moss
Situated at the far end of Moss Gate, with a pleasant, secluded car park, Risley Moss is one of the last remaining areas of post-glacial mossland in the country. It is a remnant of raised peat bog covered by sphagnum moss, which once covered the Mersey Valley from Warrington and Manchester in the north, to Knutsford in the south.

During the Industrial Revolution, farmers cleared much of the surrounding land, producing a variety of crops on the peat-rich soil. The peat-cutting industry also thrived for a time, until the 2nd World War intervened and the whole area was left to decay.

In 1975, Risley Moss was included in plans for Warrington New Town. These had three aims for the area: recreation for the people in the parkland; an education centre for school children and students to study both the social and natural history of the area, and conservation of the rare and fragile mossland. In 1980, David Bellamy performed the opening ceremony and, today, the site is a visually attractive and ecologically interesting mixture of woodland, mossland and wetland - an idyllic spot for bird watching or a woodland stroll.

An observation tower gives a grandstand view over the conserved mosses. From it, on a clear day, one can pick out Croker Hill, Shutlingsloe and other Cheshire landmarks in the Pennine foothills. Birds of prey quarter the area - kestrel, owl and sparrowhawk - while others, such as hen harrier, hobby, merlin and peregrine, pass through in Winter.

The woodland is a mixture of deciduous trees and birch, with numerous dells and coppiced areas. There are two bird hides: Peter's Hide looks out over the mossland; Woodland Hide looks onto a woodland glade, where a feeding station during the winter months is used regularly by great spotted woodpecker, nuthatch, finches and tits. Some of the ponds are ideal for pond dipping and duck are common - especially mallard, teal, snipe, woodcock and moorhen.

The wild flower meadows make ideal picnic spots and are alive with summer flowers and butterflies. In June several orchids can be found; common spotted and southern marsh are two. Because of its fragile environment access to the mossland itself is restricted. However, it contains a greater variety of species and habitats than any other place in the vicinity. At least eleven types of dragonfly breed in the pools each year and there are many wetland plants.

Risley Moss is managed as an educational nature reserve which should help its redevelopment as a living peat bog. There are toilets, information room, orienteering course and wheelchair walks. It is open every day except Friday.

The Rangers can be contacted on 0925 824339.

moorhen

AROUND CROFT

Distance:	4.5 miles
Start:	Culcheth Linear Park (SJ 649 949)
By Car:	From Warrington take the A574 towards Leigh. Turn left down Glaziers Lane before reaching Culcheth, then go right down Wigshaw Lane. After crossing the railway bridge turn sharp left to the car park in the old station.

At the Ranger cabin set off north-west into the park. After about 700 yards you pass under an old brick bridge and carry on for another 200 yards before turning left. Climb steps, then go straight ahead across fields to a country road.

Cross this and go ahead down the side of a field with a pumping station on your left. Follow the edge of the field round to your left and then descend shallow steps to the road. Turn right, then immediately left down the side of another field.

Turn left at the end of this to follow a grassy path parallel to a row of electricity pylons, veering left under these, before turning right again along a line of oaks to the next field boundary. Turn left here and walk atop a low bank, passing a solitary oak and continuing to Heath Lane. Turn right and keep right onto Lord Street at the *General Elliot* pub.

Cross the road and turn left down Abbey Close. Pass the entrance to Beacon Close and a garage, before turning left down a hidden footpath shaded by a canopy of hawthorn, where fieldfare and redwing can be seen gorging themselves on red berries in Winter, and a thick carpet of leaves deadens your footfalls.

Climb a stile at the end and continue ahead over a field. Keeping small ponds to your right you will eventually see a stile in the facing hedge. Walk over the following field and turn left along Lady Lane (away from the church). Turn right over a stile immediately before a red brick bungalow - *Lane Side*.

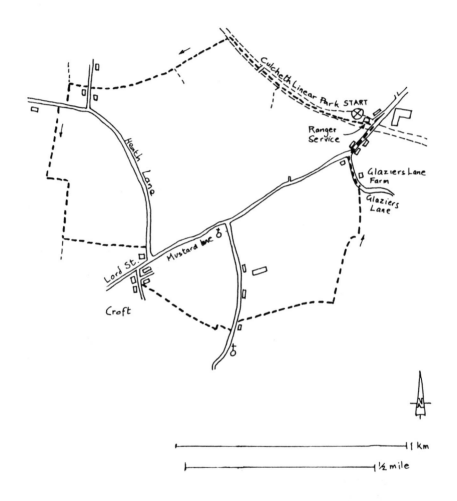

Around Croft

Follow the field edge over two stiles, then go straight ahead to a three-way signpost. Here, turn left and continue along the right-hand edge of this and the two following fields, to Glaziers Lane. Turn left, then right at Wigshaw Lane to return to Culcheth Linear Park.

Culcheth Linear Park

This follows the old Wigan to Glazebrook railway line. Almost twelve miles long, this line opened for freight in 1879, and, for passengers to Manchester or Wigan, on *April Fools' Day* five years later. 'Specials' also took racegoers to Haydock and trippers to Blackpool.

The northern end of the Park finishes at Kenyon Halt, where the railway once crossed the Manchester to Liverpool line. Adjacent to the car park, Wigshaw Lane Bridge had to be raised six feet for trains to pass under the road and, during the War, extra lines were laid from the Royal Ordnance Factory at Risley to Newchurch Halt.

The line was eventually closed in the 1968 Beeching Cuts. Oil was the last cargo to be carried regularly, taken to the Shell depot at Haydock. Most other freight traffic was, by then, being transported on the extensive motorway network.

The area soon became a muddy eyesore, but since the 1970s has been transformed into the pleasant place it is today. Alder and willow enjoy the moist conditions near the stream; oak, sycamore and silver birch are interspersed with hawthorn and gorse in cuttings, and the occasional bramble thicket offers excellent cover for small birds. Dead stumps and prone branches encourage a variety of insect life and fungi, and wildflowers enhance the meadows.

oak

Today, Culcheth Linear Park's idyllic, 1.5 mile stretch of bridleway provides peaceful walks, picnic areas and a horse ride. It also links up with an extensive footpath network.

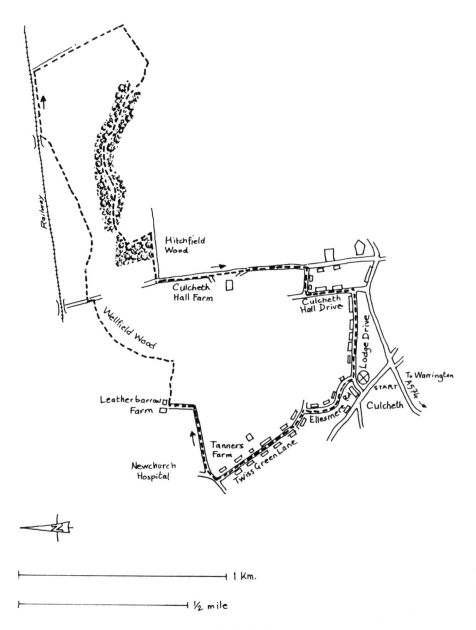

Railway

Hitchfield
Wood

Culcheth
Hall Farm

Culcheth
Hall Drive

Wellfield Wood

Lodge Drive

To Warrington

A574

START

Culcheth

Leatherbarrow
Farm

Ellesmere Rd

Tanners
Farm

Twiss Green Lane

Newchurch
Hospital

N

|———————————————————| 1 Km.

|————————————————| ½ mile

Around Culcheth

AROUND CULCHETH

Distance: 4.5 miles

Start: The shops on Lodge Drive (SJ 655 953)

By Car: From Warrington, take the A574 to Culcheth. Free parking surrounds the village centre.

From the shops turn left down Ellesmere Road, then left again down Wellfield Road, and straight on along Twiss Green Lane to Newchurch Hospital. Here, turn right through Tanner Farm, following the track to Leatherbarrow Farm.

Before the barn turn right, taking the path across the field and entering Wellfield Wood via a footbridge over the stream. Turn left and follow this permissive path through the narrow wood. At the end cross the cart bridge and turn right, following the stream to the main farm track.

Turn left towards the railway, then almost immediately right along the path by a stream. After 100 yards pass through a pinch gap at the side of a farm gate and go straight on to the right of a clump of trees. Cross the stile and follow the track to the railway, keeping the hedge on your left.

Turn right before the bridge, following the foot of the embankment. After 200 yards turn right along a hedge with a single large beech tree. Where three paths meet in the middle of a field turn right. Cross the footbridge and go over the stile on the right. Follow the field edge and cross another stile into the narrow wood.

Follow the permissive path to Hitchfield Wood. You are requested to cross the stile and follow the field edge around this wood, which is privately owned. Turn right over the stile in the corner and follow the path back to the main farm track.

Turn left here, following the path through a small paddock to the left of Culcheth Hall Farm to rejoin the track. Turn right after 300 yards and follow the narrow passage to Culcheth Hall Drive. Turn left here, returning to the village centre via Lodge Drive.

Points of Interest

In the Old English of the Saxons who felled the forest for their farms, the name Culcheth means 'on the edge of a wood'. Most names in this area are English, dating from this period of settlement between the 6th and 10th centuries.

The last Squire of Culcheth was Thomas Ellames Withington, who lived at Culcheth Hall. The house no longer stands but Culcheth Hall Drive still survives as a modern street name and avenues of grand beeches and one gate lodge (on Common Lane) have outlasted the hall itself.

A 17th century visitor to Culcheth was the adventurer and secret agent, Colonel Blood. He married a daughter of the Lord of the Manor of Culcheth and involved her in his notorious plot to steal the crown jewels.

hornbeam

Fowley Common Nothing remains of the once dense forest which covered this area but woodlands survive as pheasant shoots or old parkland or gardens and, near Fowley Common, a narrow woodland follows the brook. Many of the trees here are hornbeams, not a common tree so far north but probably planted to provide very hard timber for the machinery of flour mills. There is still a mill nearby on Warrington Road but modern machinery replaced the old tools long ago.

A PLACE TO VISIT

Pennington Flash

This lies to the north, off St. Helens Road, Leigh. It is a large lake surrounded by woodlands, wetland and open space. Activities include angling and sailing (by local clubs), golf and bird watching. Countryside Rangers are based at the Visitors' Centre. Sadly, the main car park is pay and display.

AROUND GLAZEBURY

Distance: 4 miles

Start: Raven Inn (SJ 674 961)

By Car: Take the A574 from Warrington to Glazebury. Turn right into Heyshoot Lane at the *Raven Inn* and park there.

Walk down Heyshoot Lane to the left of the inn and, after a short distance, turn left into Moss Lane. After 300 yards turn off the road over a stream and go straight ahead down the middle of a field.

When the path eventually reaches the cobbled road go straight ahead, then turn first left, passing Light Oaks Hall on your right. At the main road in Glazebury turn right. After 450 yards turn left down Hurst Lane. Follow this to Hurst Hall Farm.

Pass the front of the farmhouse and cross the stile on the left immediately before the farmyard. Follow the field edge and, taking great care, cross the railway line. Turn left and immediately right, following the hedge past a large, single beech tree.

Where three paths meet in the middle of the field, turn right. After 200 yards cross the footbridge and follow the iron railing fence to Fowley Common. At the road turn left to Warrington Road, where you turn left back to the *Raven Inn*.

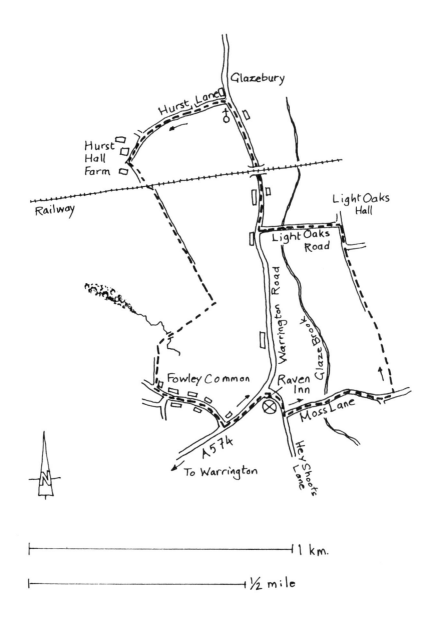

Around Glazebury

Points of Interest

The name Glazebrook has a very ancient origin: glaze, coming from the Celtic language of the Ancient Britons, meant blue-green - presumably the colour of the water at this distant time.

On this walk you cross the Liverpool to Manchester railway line, which ran the first passenger service in the world. It was opened by the Duke of Wellington in 1830 after Stephenson's *Rocket* had shown itself to be the most efficient locomotive of its time in trials on the Rainhill track.

Stephenson's Rocket

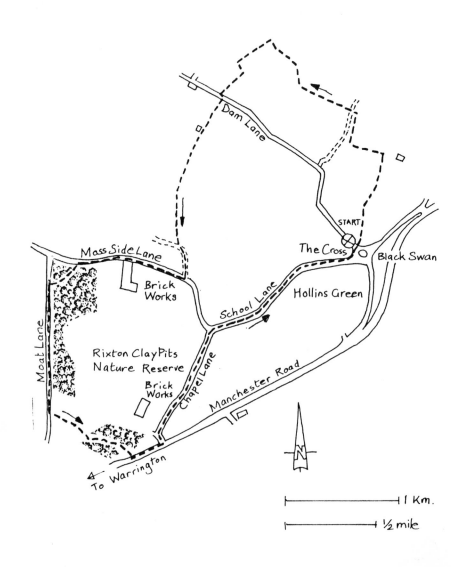

Dam Lane

START

The Cross

Black Swan

Mass Side Lane

Brick Works

Hollins Green

School Lane

Moat Lane

Rixton Clay Pits Nature Reserve

Brick Works

Chapel Lane

Manchester Road

To Warrington

N

├─────────────────┤ 1 Km.

├─────────────────┤ ½ mile

Around Rixton

AROUND RIXTON

Distance: 3.5 miles

Start: The Cross in Hollins Green (SJ 697 911)

By Car: Take the A57 (Manchester Road) from War̲ ̲
over the M6. At Hollins Green bear left onto the old road.
Pass in front of the *Eagle and Child* pub and *The Weint*,
before turning left at the *Black Swan* to park near *The Cross*.

From *The Cross* go through the pinch gap between the toilets and the
cemetery. Head for the waymark post on the hedge's right. Cross the stile
and follow the right-hand edge of the field to the waymark in the next
hedge. Turn right to the finger post on the brow of a hill.

Here turn left, following the path straight on past a poplar tree to the next
finger post. Turn right to another finger post which directs you left. Turn
left again at the next post, to cross the field with a farmhouse ahead. Cross
the ditch by the bridge and turn left, following the outside of the field to
the next waymark post.

Turn right, heading across the field towards a barn. Cross Dam Lane and
keep along the track to the barn. Go over the stile and carry on to the right
of the fence - towards the chimneys of Rixton Brick Works. Cross the
next stile and a bridge, then follow the track to Moss Side Lane.

Turn right along the lane, passing the brick works to reach a pinch gap
on the opposite (south) side of the road. Here, enter Rixton Claypits
Nature Reserve. Turn left at the information board and follow the grassy
path to Moat Lane.

Turn left and follow the road to a pinch gap with a finger post on your left.
Take the path here through the Nature Reserve to Manchester Road,
where you turn left. Turn left again into Chapel Lane before the garage.
Then a right turn at the junction into School Lane returns you to the start.

n Claypits

though industry has changed the landscape in many places it has, sometimes, helped wildlife to survive. At Rixton, old pits left after clay extraction for brickmaking, remain as a patchwork of woods, damp meadows and open water, the alkaline clay allowing orchids and yellow wort to grow.

These abandoned clay workings, last dug in the 1960s by Irlam Brickworks, have enabled Rixton Claypits to become an SSSI. The reserve comprises several lakes interspersed with islands, reedbeds and willow scrub, all rich in wildlife. Because of its varied topography and rich soil, it provides a wildlife refuge in an area dominated by light industry and agriculture.

Huge numbers of plant and bird species can be found. These include more than 200 plants: marsh and common spotted orchids, yellow wort, common centaury, stoneworts - all at their best in June, plus many types of autumnal fungi. A wildflower meadow is also being sown.

Hundreds of birds can be seen. Look out for willow and sedge warblers, willow tits, whitethroat and ruddy duck. Insect life also thrives: many butterflies and nine species of dragonfly breed here. Common, pygmy and water shrew also inhabit the area; the common frog abounds and there is a large colony of the rare, great crested newt.

Parking in Moat Lane, off the A57 (Manchester Road), the visitor can enjoy woodland and waterside walks on the plethora of footpaths which meander around the reserve.

The site is managed by the Warrington Borough Council Rangers, who may be contacted on 0925 601617.

common spotted orchid

AROUND WOOLSTON

Distance: 6.5 miles

Start: Junction of Weir Lane and Manchester Road (SJ 656 892)

By Car: Take the A57 (Manchester Road) east from Warrington. Before reaching the M6 turn right into Weir Lane at a small war memorial and park at the roadside.

Follow Weir Lane down to the River Mersey, veering right to pass a cottage, once the lock keeper's home, then almost immediately left to cross the river on a flat footbridge. Follow the new path up the far bank and bear right along its top to the Manchester Ship Canal. Below are the remains of the old weir, which has recently been replaced. Downriver, a suspension bridge spans the river's original course.

Keep ahead, then turn right and follow the track alongside the Manchester Ship Canal for a mile or so, to Latchford Locks. Here, the track becomes Thelwall Lane. Follow this and then turn second right into Nook Lane. Bear left along Marsden Avenue and, at the end, carry on across playing fields to the river.

Here turn left, following Mersey Walk and then a footpath, keeping the river on the right. At Kingsway Bridge cross the river and turn down the ramp onto the opposite bank. Turn left, following the riverside path behind the allotments. (This path is part of the *Mersey Way*.)

Follow the railings along Paddington Bank to the right until you reach a gap through to the river again. Turn right across the old locks to follow the riverside path. After a mile or so the path joins a road. Cross over the New Cut Canal and turn right along the towpath, which takes you back to Weir Lane.

Latchford Locks

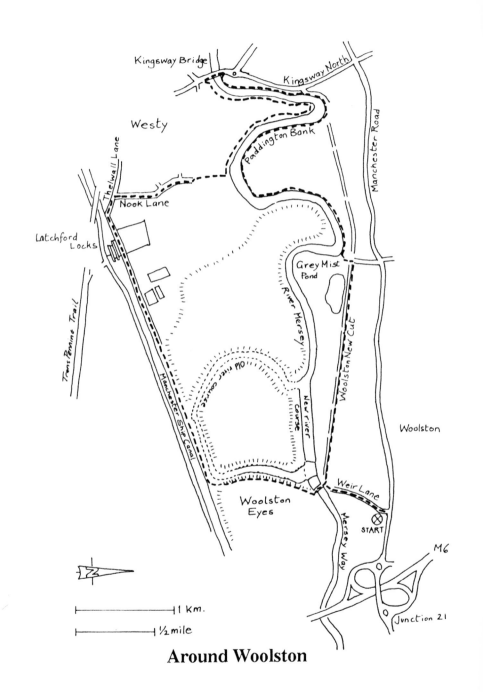

Kingsway Bridge

Kingsway North

Westy

Paddington Bank

Manchester Road

Thelwall Lane

Nook Lane

Latchford Locks

Trans Pennine Trail

Grey Mist Pond

River Mersey

Woolston New Cut

Manchester Ship Canal

Old River Course

New River Course

Woolston

Woolston Eyes

Weir Lane

START

Mersey Way

M6

Junction 21

N

1 Km.

½ mile

Around Woolston

Waterways

Until the coming of the railways, water provided the main trade links between Manchester and the sea. The **River Mersey** was shallow as it meandered between Woolston and Thelwall village. However, from the 1700s attempts were made to make the journey along the river shorter and quicker.

Shortcuts were dug; the most recent was the Woolston New Cut, only recently abandoned and silted up. Weirs on the river held deep water upstream and fed canals. The weirs remain and help combat pollution by adding oxygen to the water as it flows over them.

In the 1890s, the **Manchester Ship Canal** was dug, allowing deep-water craft to sail up to Manchester and making the River Mersey redundant as a waterway for transport.

At **Woolston Eyes**, enormous dumping grounds for the silt from the Manchester Ship Canal provide artificial marshlands for vast numbers of ducks, waders and gulls, particularly in Winter.

A PLACE TO VISIT

Woolston Park

This large open space follows Spittle Brook down to the River Mersey. There are several entrances, including one on Manchester Road near Paddington post office, but the main car park is off Hillock Lane.

The 56-acre park, opened in 1977, and was created by Warrington New Town from derelict farmland. In the same year a garden was planted with roses with royal names, to celebrate the Queen's Silver Jubilee.

heron

There are also wildflower meadows, woods melodious with birdsong and a pond with mallards, moorhens and a breeding pair of swans. A kingfisher pays frequent visits there and long tailed tits nest nearby. You may also see a jay, little grebe or heron.

Spring flowers provide bright splashes of colour throughout the parkland: snowdrops followed by crocus, primrose, daffodil and cowslip. Other flowers are birdsfoot trefoil, scarlet pimpernel, the tiny field pansy and wood sorrel.

A children's playground is equipped with plenty of adventurous equipment and, for the fitness fanatic, a Trim Track is supposed to exercise every part of the body! On a Sunday in early summer *Beating the Bounds* has become a popular annual event for all the family, when a six mile walk round the parish is followed by a fun festival in the park.

For more information about Woolston Park contact the Ranger Service there on 0925 824398.

WARRINGTON AND THE NORTH

Burtonwood	Victoria Park
Latchford	Wilderspool
Sankey	Winwick

Coal Tips and Cotton Grass

Around Burtonwood and Winwick coal measures underlie much of the landscape and, until recently, there was an active pit at Newton, its two concrete towers visible from afar. Colliery spoil heaps rear above the flat farmland, although the last few decades have seen many of these grassed over, with help from fertilizers and fast-growing varieties of trees and grasses. Much of the older landscape survives though, mainly as agricultural tracts dotted with small woodlands. There is even a piece of peat bog to the north of Burtonwood, with its special flora of mosses, purple moor grass and white-headed cotton grass.

Warrington's Waterways

Visitors to Warrington, especially walkers, are often confused by the waterways that they cross and recross. The River Mersey in particular meanders through the town and navigation projects of the 18th and 19th centuries have changed the route, sometimes leaving sections of the old meanders still intact.

Warrington grew because of its position - first as a fording place of the River Mersey (at Latchford), then later as an important bridging point. Waterways were vital too to Warrington's industrial growth, and to the west of the town five navigation routes run parallel, including the first and last of the English Canal Age. These are: the St. Helens Canal (Sankey Navigation), the River Mersey, the Runcorn and Latchford Canal, the Bridgewater Canal and the Manchester Ship Canal. The walks in this section follow four of these waterways.

The River Mersey has always been tidal up to Howley Weir and, until 1740, only small boats could come further upstream than Bank Quay because of its shallowness. The Mersey and Irwell Navigation Act allowed Manchester businessmen to improve navigation up to Manchester, constructing locks, cuts and weirs to keep up the water level. Howley Lock and Weir survive from this period and can be seen as you walk through Victoria Park, and much of the *Mersey Way* uses the towpath formed at this time.

One of the later straightening projects moved the river from Wilderspool Causeway to what is now Chester Road. The walk around Wilderspool follows part of the old route here and, from Greenalls Avenue, you may see part of this section which was retained as Warrington Lock - a link between the river and the Manchester Ship Canal. Also on this walk the link is viewed from the other side, as the path goes between the River Mersey and the Runcorn to Latchford Canal.

The Runcorn and Latchford Canal opened in 1807 - an answer to the Mersey's problems of low tides and sandbanks. The surviving section of this is seen on the Wilderspool walk, although both the Latchford and the Victoria Park routes follow its line through Black Bear Park. This was the last section of this canal to fall out of use, staying open between the River Mersey at Manor Lock, Kingsway, and the Ship Canal at Stockton Heath, until the mid-1970s. It was known as the Black Bear Canal after the pub on Knutsford Road which is passed on the Latchford walk.

The Manchester Ship Canal opened in 1894, allowing ocean-going vessels to reach Manchester for the first time. Despite its situation 43 miles inland, and competition from the then extensive railway network, Manchester became Britain's third-largest port . Trade declined as cargo vessels became too wide and deep for Latchford Locks.

Strange invaders

Several plants foreign to this area have got a hold on the river banks and canal sides.

Perhaps the prettiest is the Himalayan balsam, the sweet-scented blooms of which you will find along much of the River Mersey throughout the Summer. This plant might shock you too, with its habit of shooting off its exploding seed capsules as you brush against it.

Himalayan balsam

Next to the balsam you will usually find the fast-growing Japanese knotweed, a plant related to the Russian vine but standing stoutly on its own enormous stems. Its flowers are insignificant but you will recognise it by its long, heart-shaped leaves.

Tall plants with large globes of white flowers and green seeds may well be sweet angelica - but beware! - they can be confused with the irritating and poisonous giant hogweed.

You are also likely to find plants introduced by humans on your walks by the waterways. Some are survivors from garden rubbish but others have seeded themselves. Apt for a brewing town, the rough stemmed hop is found climbing over several fences and hedgerows, and there is even a fig tree on the north bank of the River Mersey by Howley Quay.

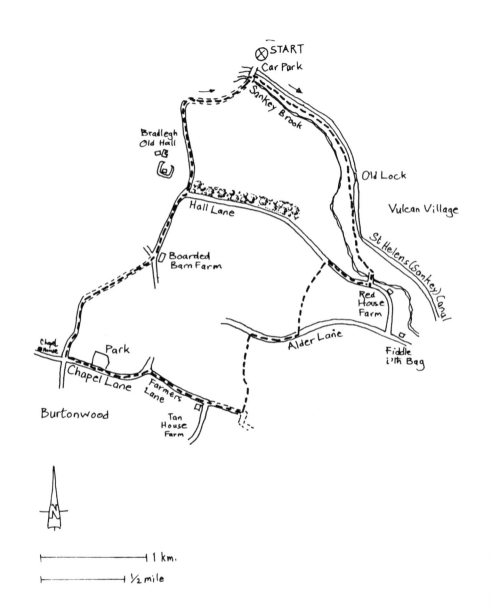

Around Burtonwood

AROUND BURTONWOOD

Distance: 4 miles

Start: Red Brow Wood, near Vulcan village (SJ 577 944)

By Car: Take the A49 north from Warrington. At Winwick church turn left at traffic lights towards Burtonwood. Just before a railway bridge turn right down Alder Root Lane. Continue into Vulcan village. After passing the *Wargrave Inn* and the parish church, turn left into Bradlegh Road. Then bear right to the car park at Red Brow Wood.

Cross the Sankey Canal at the now fixed swing bridge and turn left along the towpath. After passing the filled-in locks continue for 200 yards or so, before turning right off the towpath through a pinch gap. Then walk across the field and over a bridge to Hall Lane.

Turn right down the lane to Hall Lane Farm, then turn left off the road and follow the field's edge. Go through a back garden and keep Stoneyard Cottages to your left. Walk up the drive and through the gate.

Turn right down Alder Lane, then left off the road just before Alder Lane Farm. Follow the waymarked route through the fields to the track. Turn right down this and carry on down Farmers Lane, then turn left down Chapel Lane.

Continue almost to the church, then turn right, following the track to the road at Boarded Barn Farm. Cross the road and go down Hall Lane (referred to locally as Gypsy Wood). At the first bend turn left down a track, to pass Bradlegh Old Hall. Veer right round a bend, then walk downhill to Sankey Valley. Cross the bridge over Sankey Brook and ahead is the canal and your starting point.

Points of Interest

The St. Helens' Rangers look after the northern section of the Sankey Valley from St. Helens to Burtonwood. They are based at the Visitors' Centre on Blackbrook Road, St. Helens. (Telephone: 0744 39252.)

The quarry which now forms the car park at Red Brow Wood provided stone for the nine-arched Sankey Viaduct. Built in 1830 by George Stephenson at a cost of £45,000, it was the first passenger railway in the world, and transported people between Liverpool and Manchester.

The Mucky Mountains, which rise to the north west of the car park, are the spoil heaps of alkaline waste from a soda factory which operated here - long since closed down. Much wildlife has now colonised on them, including quaking grass, and pyramid and northern marsh orchids.

In 1757 the **Sankey Navigation** became the first still water canal in England. Parallel to it runs the **Sankey Brook**, once a clear trout stream which became so foully polluted by industry that it was nicknamed the Stinking Brook.

Many locomotives were built at the **Vulcan** foundry during the heyday of our railways and Vulcan village was built to house the workforce. Today, *Rushton Diesels* operate from the works and their wide ventilator chimneys can be seen from afar.

Bradlegh Old Hall, surrounded by a fine moat and guarded by a 15th century gatehouse, is steeped in history and is one of the oldest buildings in the area. These features remain from its time as home of Sir Piers Legh, an ancient Lord of the Manor, but today's farmhouse was rebuilt in the 17th century from the stones of the old hall.

Stories of ghosts and secret passages still abound and several unusual artefacts can be found inside. Late in the 15th century Richard, Duke of Gloucester (later to become Richard III) stayed here on his way to take Berwick Castle and repel the Scots. In the King's Room, the seven-foot-long, oaken four-poster in which he slept, remains intact, its measurements roughly carved in Roman numerals.

AROUND LATCHFORD

Distance: 5 miles

Start: Kingsway Bridge (SJ 625 880)

By Car: Take the A57 east from Warrington town centre. Turn right into Farrell Street at traffic lights before the parish church. Bear right at a roundabout, cross Kingsway Bridge, then park in any wide side street.

Walk back to the bridge, where the walk starts to the east of the road (furthest away from Warrington). Go down the ramp towards the river and turn left. Walk under the bridge, either using the track or the cantilevered towpath. Continue towards the remains of Manor Lock.

Turn left now and follow Black Bear Park along the route of the filled-in Runcorn to Latchford Canal. Pass under Knutsford Road, a railway bridge and Loushers Lane, where open ground to the left allows you to reach the Manchester Ship Canal.

Turn left and follow the canal, mid mounds of glorious gorse, towards the high level, Cantilever Bridge. Take the last cut through on the left before the football ground with its floodlights. Then turn right along Pearson Avenue and keep right up onto Station Road and over the bridge.

Turn immediately right again down the ramp to Fairfield Road beneath. Cross this road and turn right. As the road bends to the right take the footpath to the left, following the Ship Canal along Greenbank Road to the next swing bridge at Knutsford Road.

Cross Knutsford Road onto Thelwall New Road and continue to follow the canal for half-a-mile, walking under the skew railway bridge, to Latchford Locks. Turn left here through the gap in the fence and cross the Ship Canal by the lock gates.

On the other side of the locks turn left into Thelwall Lane. Follow this and then take the second right turn into Nook Lane. Bear left along Marsden Avenue and, at the end, veer left again across the playing fields to the

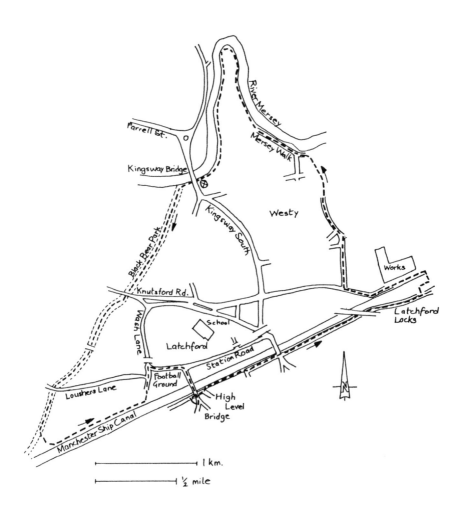

Farrell St.

River Mersey

Mersey Walk

Kingsway Bridge

Kingsway South

Westy

Black Bear Park

Knutsford Rd.

Works

Latchford Locks

Wash Lane

School

Latchford

Station Road

Football Ground

Loushers Lane

High Level Bridge

Manchester Ship Canal

N

├───────────────┤ 1 km.

├───────────────┤ ½ mile

Around Latchford

river. Here turn left, to follow Mersey Walk and then a footpath. Keep the river on your right to return to Kingsway Bridge.

Points of Interest

The soaring spire of **St. Elfin's** parish church dominates the town. The third tallest church spire in England, it was only added to this ancient church in 1860. Crowned with a weather cock gilded with golden sovereigns, the Rector at that time devised a slogan 'a guinea for a golden cock' to raise funds to pay for it.

You may also be lucky enough to hear the mellow notes of the eight computerised bells which are sometimes programmed to play a hymn tune as they strike the hour.

Latchford was the place where an ancient ford crossed the River Mersey long before it was bridged at Bridge Foot. In 1934, the ferro-concreted **Kingsway Bridge** provided Warrington with its second road crossing of the river.

Many of the roads near this bridge have been named after the network of waterways (river, canals and brooks) which create so many transport problems in the town. Some of these are: Bridgewater Avenue, Worsley Avenue, Morris Avenue, Brook Avenue and Mersey Walk.

The imposing, high-level **skew bridge** crossing the Manchester Ship Canal at Latchford was on the Warrington to Altrincham railway line, which opened in 1840 and was closed during the Beeching Cuts of 1962. From its station at Arpley the line's construction involved considerable gradient work and much of its route is now an attractive section of the Trans-Pennine Trail.

In 1906, the **Richmond Works** started trading opposite Latchford Locks and, by 1947, had produced over a million gas cookers. The works still produce cookers here, but under a different name - *New World*.

Nearby are the Latchford Workshops. The brick tower houses an accumulator, and the hydraulic pumping station operates both the locks and Warrington's three swing bridges.

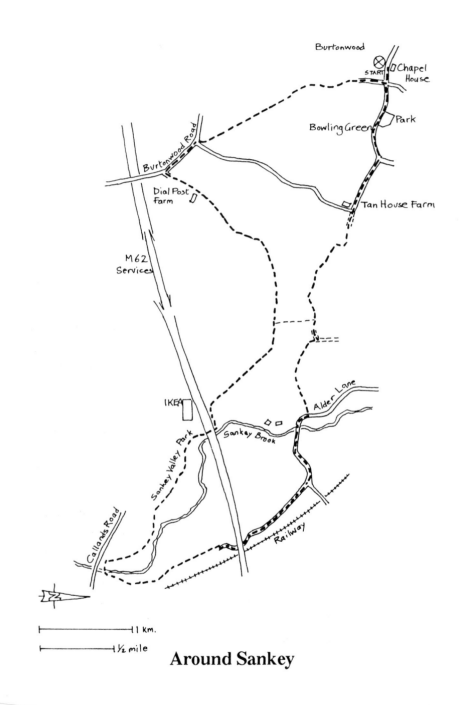

Burtonwood

START ⊗ 🏠 Chapel House

Park

Bowling Green

Burtonwood Road

Burtonwood Road

Tan House Farm

Dial Post Farm 🏠

M62 Services

Alder Lane

IKEA

Sankey Valley Park

Sankey Brook

Callands Road

Railway

⊢───────⊣ 1 km.

⊢───────⊣ ½ mile

Around Sankey

AROUND SANKEY

Distance: 6 miles

Start: *Chapel House* pub in Burtonwood (SJ 564 928)

By Car: Take the A57 (Sankey Way) west from Warrington and follow the signs for Burtonwood. Keep ahead at the first traffic lights, bear right at a roundabout, then right at traffic lights along Whittle Avenue, which becomes Burtonwood Road. In Burtonwood village turn left into the *Chapel House* car park. (Groups should check with the licensee beforehand.)

Turn left out of the car park, then right down a path by the parish hall. Follow the path to a track, which you cross, then walk over fields to Tan House Lane. Turn right, then left onto Burtonwood Road.

Turn left down the farm track just before the road rises. Follow this track to Dial Post Farm. Go through the farmyard and follow a waymark east along the field edge. At the three-way sign go straight on. Continue through the gap in the hedge (by the pylon), then walk across the field to a track. (Aim for the tree in the middle.)

Keep ahead down the track and under the M62. Then follow gravel paths through Sankey Valley Park, keeping Sankey Brook to the left. Go over five wooden bridges and cross the concrete footbridge over Sankey Brook (near Callands Road).

Head north towards the railway footbridge down the gravel path, turning left just before the next wooden footbridge. Keep to the high ground until you reach a track at the old canal building with 1841 written on its side.

Follow this track under the M62, past the scrap yard and down to Alder Lane, where you turn left. 50 yards after crossing Sankey Brook turn left down the track and follow it to Farmers Lane. Go straight down this lane and a left turn down Chapel Lane will take you back to the pub.

Look carefully at the Chapel House pub sign, then have a look at the church next door to spot the difference.

The Sankey Navigation (St. Helens Canal) was the first canal of the English Canal Age, opening in November 1757, two years before the Bridgewater Canal. The Sankey Navigation claimed to be a rationalisation of the Sankey Brook, rather than a new canal, a ploy to get permission through Parliament with less opposition.

The Sankey Canal was built to facilitate the transport of coal from the St. Helens area to Liverpool and was in use until the 1960s. Coal from Newton's collieries and sugar from the Sankey Sugar Refinery were two of the main cargoes, the last load of sugar travelling upstream to Earlstown in 1959. Sections of the canal have now been restored but others have been filled in completely, only traceable by the outline of edging stone.

Canal craft were usually called by girls' names and each company sported its own distinctive colours. Even during the early part of this century whole families lived on the canal and a round trip from Liverpool to St. Helens would take anything from two to five days, depending on weather, tides and traffic.

Today, the canal is popular with fishermen, canoeists, walkers and wildlife enthusiasts. To the north, **Bewsey Lock** has some interesting features, including its datestone, the recess for the lock gates and some mooring bollards.

The **Seven Arches** viaduct, designed by Stephenson and built by the Cheshire Lines Committee in 1873, has foundations containing bales of cotton waste. Metal plates fixed to the corners of the abutments protected the bridge from the continual rubbing from the ropes of horse-drawn boats; grooves in the plates are still visible. The structure's high, square span facilitated the tall masts of Mersey flats.

The **Sankey Way** crosses the canal at Buttermilk Swing Bridge. Originally, the canal only extended to Sankey Bridges, where a lock gave access to the River Mersey. Here too the busy rail link between Warrington and Widnes once crossed the canal on a swing bridge. As boats had right-of-way this was normally left open, as a result of which an engine fell into the canal and a ghost train is supposed to haunt the spot on the anniversary of the event. The platform at Sankey Halt can still be seen and nearby is the *Sloop Inn* which once provided bargees with a well-earned pint.

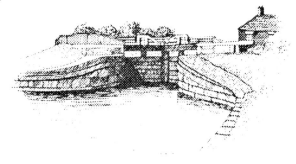

Old Lock

A PLACE TO VISIT

Sankey Valley Park

The Sankey Canal is the focal point of this linear park. Its Cheshire section, which stretches south from Bewsey Bridge to Sankey Bridges, incorporates walks, picnic places, climbing frames, a wildfowl reserve, angling and, in summer, a butterfly garden boasting at least 15 species. These include: red admiral, common blue and small copper. There are also 180 different kinds of trees and shrubs to enjoy.

Surrounded by its abandoned moat, **Bewsey Old Hall** dates back to the 15th century, its history littered with tales of mystery and murder. One early story tells of Sir John Boteler who, in December 1430, was killed by the Earl of Derby's assassins while in bed. His son was smuggled to safety by his nurse. Blood stains still splotch the bedroom floor and the ghost of his wife, the white lady, can be seen to this day wandering around the lonely mansion!

To reach the park, take the A57 (Sankey Way) from Warrington, then turn right at traffic lights onto Cromwell Way. Turn right at the first roundabout to a screened car park. Rangers can be contacted at Bewsey Old Hall on 0925 571836.

AROUND VICTORIA PARK

Distance: 2.5 miles

Start: Victoria Park (SJ 617 876)

By Car: Take the A50 (Knutsford Road) east from Bridge Foot in
Warrington. At the main entrance to Victoria Park turn left
to a large car park.

Walk back to Knutsford Road and turn right to Bridge Foot. Cross the
River Mersey by the war memorial and turn right. Cross Mersey Street
and immediately turn down Wharfe Street, along the Howley side of the
River Mersey and away from Warrington's town centre.

Keep to the riverside path, past Howley Lock and Weir, until you reach
a suspension bridge. Cross the river on this footbridge and turn left, then
follow the riverside path to the remains of Manor Lock.

Here turn right into Black Bear Park - the route of the filled-in Runcorn
to Latchford Canal. After a few hundred yards take any right-hand
entrance into Victoria Park, strolling through the gardens and enjoying
the open space before arriving back at your starting point.

The **River Mersey** became navigable as far upstream as Warrington late
in the 17th century. Following on from this Howley Quay was built in
1761 and is reputed to be the oldest up-river wharf in the North West.
Warehouses were quickly established along its banks, some of which
still remain today.

The lock at Howley Cut was built to provide access past the weir for boats
going upstream. It is a good example of early civil engineering. Nearby,
Howley suspension footbridge was opened in 1912 - a boon for those
living in Latchford and working in Warrington.

Victoria Park was originally the *Old Warps* estate. Purchased by the
Borough Council in 1896, it was then renamed after Queen Victoria. The
family mansion used to be a maternity home and is now a nursing home.

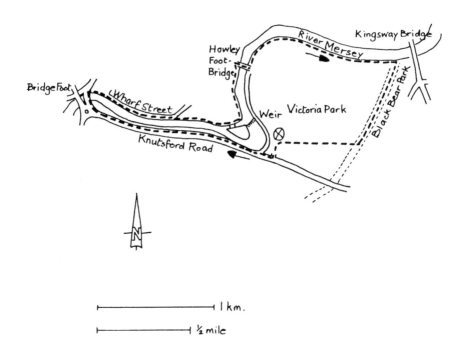

Around Victoria Park

AROUND WILDERSPOOL

Distance: 5 miles

Start: St. Thomas' church, Stockton Heath (SJ 613 864)

By Car: Take the A49 south from Warrington. Cross the swing bridge into Stockton Heath, then turn right by the *Red Lion* into West Avenue. Turn right again and find a space at the far end of the car park.

Cut through the snicket past toilets and church. Turn left and cross the swing bridge. Then straightaway, turn left again and walk on the footpath alongside the Manchester Ship Canal. Keep along here 'midst banks of bluebells, honesty, brambles and nettles, until the path bears right between allotments to Wilderspool Crescent.

Turn left here and, at the end, cross the road to a path. Bear slightly left along this, aiming for the far end of the old course of the River Mersey. Carry on with this on your left, passing locks, then following the remains of the Runcorn to Latchford Canal to Chester Road.

Cross this with care and turn left over the iron bridge. Immediately, descend steps on your right with timber handrails. From the bottom of these take the path which lies to the right, between the River Mersey and the Runcorn to Latchford Canal.

At the railway bridge cross the river on the high footbridge, then go under railway bridges and walk along the riverside path. Before the first road bridge turn right to follow a waymarked path. This joins a road which passes under the railway then rises onto Slutchers Lane. Cross this and turn right.

(Hopefully, the footpath which once went left to the railway bridge at Bridge Foot from here will soon be reinstated.) For the present, turn left, walking through *The Village* complex to the new, blue bridge. Cross this and turn right. At the far side of the roundabout use the pedestrian crossing over Chester Road.

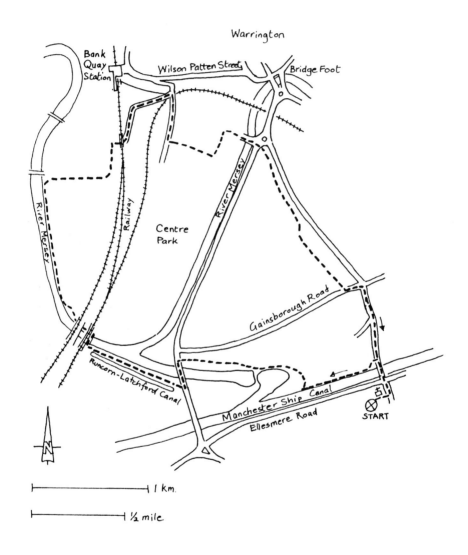

Around Wilderspool

Follow the footpath across the grass opposite, then continue down the narrow road between houses and railings, and behind the old malt kiln with its diamond panes. At the community centre go to the right-hand side of railings and follow the green space through to Gainsborough Road. (You have in fact followed the old route of the River Mersey.)

Cross the road here and turn left to crossroads, where you turn right along the A49. Walk back to Stockton Heath along this, passing a terrace of houses built for brewery workers, the end of Greenall's Avenue, the *Saracen's Head* pub and Greenall's now-defunct brewery.

Points of Interest

In 1837 the Crewe to Warrington railway line was opened, incorporating the handsome twelve-arched viaduct at **Arpley**. Built of red sandstone (now somewhat grimy), this line was part of the Grand Junction Railway from Birmingham to Warrington.

Bank Quay replaced an earlier station in Dallam Lane and has been considerably altered over the years. The area has been an industrial site since the River Mersey was made navigable to this point at the end of the 17th century. Looming above the station is Joseph Crosfield's famous soapworks. Founded in 1814 and now a reluctant part of Unilever, it still manufactures several well-known products, such as *Persil* and *Domestos*.

Crosfields' Transporter Bridge was the only one of its type built for rail traffic. It was also the last transporter bridge in the world to be constructed. Its main function was to carry single trucks from the Crosfields' works on the north bank of the River Mersey to the other plant on the Cheshire side. It was in use from 1916 to 1964 but still stands as a listed 'building'.

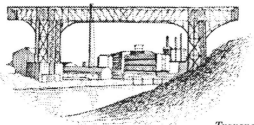

Transporter

Wilderspool, in its heyday as an industrial Roman settlement, produced articles of pottery, glass and metalwork, probably selling many of these to the garrison town at Chester (Deva).

Greenall's Avenue was on the main route from Wilderspool to Chester for nearly 2,000 years, in fact until the cutting of the Manchester Ship Canal, after which it became a quiet backwater.

Brewing was set up commercially in the town by Thomas Greenall in 1786. The *Saracen's Head*, on Wilderspool Causeway, was the original brewhouse but, as the business grew, a larger brewery was constructed across the road.

In the 19th century, the grandson of Thomas, Gilbert, brought three nephews from the Whitley side of the family into the business - hence the name, Greenall Whitley. Gilbert Greenall was also a very popular Member of Parliament for Warrington for many years and was knighted for his services to the town.

AROUND WINWICK

Distance: 4.5 miles

Start: *The Swan* in Winwick village (SJ 605 928)

By Car: Take the A49 north from Warrington. Cross over the M62 and, at the next roundabout, continue towards Newton-le-Willows. Bear right into Golborne Road (in front of Winwick Church) and the pub car park is on your right. Use the top car park and groups should check with the licensee.

From the *The Swan* turn left and follow the road left at the roundabout. After about 100 yards cross the road and climb over a stile. Go straight on to a three-way sign and turn left down a grassy track. Follow this south towards the M62.

Cross the motorway by the footbridge and turn left towards Peel Hall Farm. Go through the farmyard and follow the track (Radley Lane). Cross the road at the end of this and take the path between *The Plough* and the houses.

Go up the steps and turn left down the road. After 200 yards turn right into a field. Turn left after 50 yards, heading north. Turn right at the waymark sign and then left over the first stile. Follow waymarks around a grassy hollow and go through the wood over two stiles.

Turn left down the lane and turn right up Southworth Lane. Cross the road and turn left down steps just before the motorway. Climb over the stile and follow the edge of the field to the next stile. Then turn left down to Highfield Lane. Turn right up the lane and cross the dual carriageway at the end.

From here, walk up Waterworks Lane and turn right onto the footpath at the bend in the road. Go down the path, turning left at the end down Golborne Road and back to the car park.

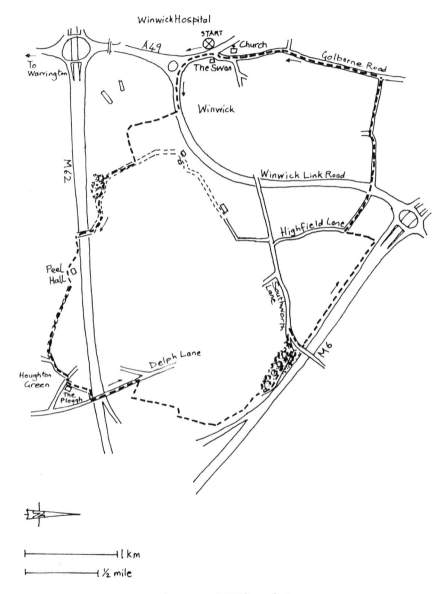

Around Winwick

Battles and Saints

Way back in time, the Winwick area was the frontier in the wars between the Saxon kingdoms of Mercia and Northumbria. Oswald, king of the latter, is said to have died in battle at Winwick. As one of the first Christian kings Oswald became a Saint, and a hermit kept watch over the holy well where he had his last drink. The hermit is commemorated by a pub and by Hermitage Lane, but St. Oswald had a fine church named after him ...

St. Oswald's Church, Winwick

The ancient church of St. Oswald dates from 1358, although an earlier church on the site is mentioned in the Domesday Book. The church has many interesting features and an excellent guidebook.

Winwick Church

Legend says that one night a pig moved the building stone of the church to the true site of St. Oswald's burial place. Medieval carvings of St. Oswald and the pig may be seen in the church. Outside, on the tower wall a pig also stands beside St. Anthony, whether because a pig was the saint's mascot, or this was the builder's cryptic way of putting the intials of St. Oswald's, Winwick, (SOW), on the building, is open to conjecture.

There were also skirmishes at Winwick in the English Civil Wars of the 1600s, when the Royalist Scottish troops were eventually defeated by Cromwell and surrendered in Warrington. The post office opposite the church was once an ale house, said to have been used by Cromwell's army as its headquarters during the battle of Preston in 1648.

Around Winwick

On the green opposite *The Swan* is a **Traveller's Rest**, donated by Sir Gilbert Greenall in 1860. Inscribed on the stone seat are, appropriately enough, the words: I will look towards thy sanctuary while I am here.

Winwick Hospital cared for the sick in both World Wars and was probably the largest military hospital in England at that time. Opposite its main gate is the site of **Delph Quarry**, the subject of legends, of tunnels said to run from the quarry to Winwick Church, and of a cave where Oliver Cromwell is supposed to have rested in 1648.

Peel Hall Park has ponds, woods and bridleways, and there is a car park off Greenwood Crescent in Orford.

Peel Hall, which retains its Georgian character and gave the area its name, stands near the site of a 12th century, medieval moated manor house, and the moat's outline can still be traced.

An old Quaker Mission House stands on the outskirts of Houghton Green and, on the other side of the motorway, Spa Well House was the home of the Titanic's captain when it sank on its final, fatal voyage.

1774 is the date on *The Plough*'s foundation stone, but an older pub may have stood on the site. At the back stood the constable's cottage and, hidden in its rafters, records were found of tithes paid to the Royalists by such eminent families as The Botelers of Bewsey Hall, the Egertons of Tatton, and others.

Myddleton Hall dates back to 1658. One of the few genuinely old houses still standing, it is a handsome building of handmade bricks.

Bronze Age barrows (burial mounds), now difficult to spot on either side of Highfield Lane, date back 3,000 years. Excavated in 1859, unearthed relics included stone hammer heads, bronze spear heads and burial urns. These are now in Warrington Museum.

SOUTH OF WARRINGTON

Appleton Thorn	Oughtrington
Grappenhall	Stockton Heath
Lymm	Thelwall

Map
The relevant map for these six walks is Warrington (SJ 68/78).

Landscape
10,000 years ago the Ice Age left behind a covering of fertile clay here over the older well-drained sandstone. Dense forest developed until it was cleared for farmland by the Saxons, and the area was well settled by medieval times.

Today, woodlands survive as shelter belts, pheasant shoots, or on the steep banks (or *bongs*) of streams. These often flow through dingles they have cut in the sandstone as they drop down to join the River Mersey or, for the last 100 years, the Manchester Ship Canal.

pheasant

Old Stone
A ridge of red sandstone rises south of the River Mersey, growing steadily higher from Lymm and Grappenhall in the west as far as Frodsham and Helsby in the east. This characterises the landscape here and many vantage points provide the walker with panoramic views over the nearby countryside and towns. The sandstone itself was the material from which the many parish churches were built, and it was also used for the walls of older farms and estates.

Old Woods

This area has some very productive farmland but woodlands also survive as landscaped gardens, pheasant shoots, or valley sides too steep to farm, as is the case with the dingles at Appleton and Lymm. The big houses of the Georgian and Victorian estates no longer exist but their landscape survives, such as the skyline plantation of pines between Grappenhall and Appleton, and the woodland of Broom Cottage among the new houses of Dudlow's Green.

Like many of our country's small woodlands these have suffered from neglect, rhododendron and sycamore shading out all woodland flowers and shrubs, and no new trees replacing the mature ones as they died and fell. However today, the woodlands provide valuable homes for wildlife - for birds, mammals, insects, wild flowers and shrubs - and management work now ensures their survival.

Old Roads

This area has one of Cheshire's oldest roads in London Road (the A49). This was the Roman road south from the industrial settlement at Wilderspool. It survived as a medieval route and later as a busy coach road.

The modern A49 does not follow the Roman road exactly and on the Appleton Thorn and Stockton Heath walks you can follow quieter sections of the old route. Also on the Appleton Thorn walk another ancient track, Green Lane, will give an idea of what the main roads might have been like in medieval England.

Old Names

Old English names abound in this area and several places appear in the Domesday Book - the Norman inventory of English settlements compiled in the 11th century. Appleton and Grappenhall both appear, Appleton being valued at 16 shillings and Grappenhall at five or six. Both were held by a free man called Dot. (As pronunciation and spelling changed, could this be the *Dood* of Dood's Lane on the Appleton Thorn and Stockton Heath walks?)

AROUND APPLETON THORN

Distance: 5 miles

Start: Appleton Thorn (SJ 638 838)

By Car: Take the A49 south from Warrington. At the Stretton traffic lights turn left onto the B5356. Park in the large lay-by as you approach Appleton Thorn.

Turn left towards the church. At the crossroads turn sharp left, past the church and huge Victorian vicarage, into Green Lane. You soon pass a black-and-white cottage, dated 1630 and once a farmhouse.

Continue along this lane until it meets Dood's Lane. Then turn left, following a footpath sign over a bridge and a stile, into the corner of a field. Cross another stile to the right and follow waymarks until you enter the young woodland of a new park.

Join the surfaced path and follow this to the left onto Cann Lane. Turn left and walk for 400 yards, crossing to a footpath marked on the right. Go over the stile and follow waymarks, keeping left until you come out on Stretton Road, where you turn right to the church.

Turn left opposite the church down Spark Hall Close, which follows the line of the old Roman road and brings you to the motorway roundabout. With great care cross the roundabout keeping left, then take the Northwich Road (A559).

After about 300 yards turn left into Well Lane and follow this as it bears right to become Mosshall Lane. Just before Mosshall Farm turn left following waymark arrows. Turn left again as soon as the path branches and follow this path over the motorway.

After the bridge turn right over the stile. Follow this path alongside the motorway for 800 yards, climbing over more stiles until you find a waymarked path to the left. This path will take you to Pepper Street, where you then turn right and return to Appleton Thorn.

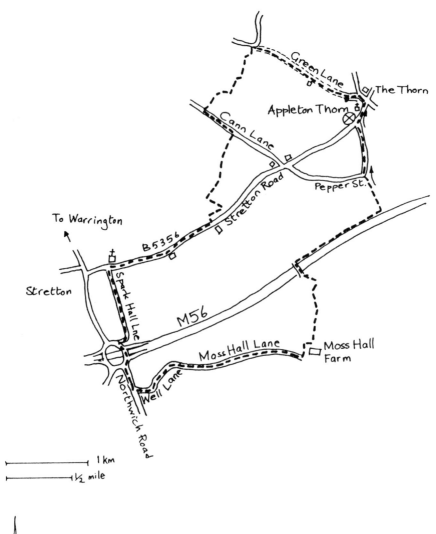

Green Lane

The Thorn

Appleton Thorn

Cann Lane

Pepper St.

Stretton Road

To Warrington

B5356

Stretton

Spark Hall Lne

M56

Moss Hall Lane

Moss Hall Farm

Well Lane

Northwich Road

1 km

½ mile

N

Around Appleton Thorn

Points of Interest

The remains of **Appleton Cross** can be seen at the junction of Cann Lane and Stretton Road. Although such crosses probably originated as pulpits for outdoor preachers, in the Middle Ages these usually marked the site of a regular market. As at other places such as Lymm and Chester, one of the roads meeting at the cross here is Pepper Street. In those days, spices such as pepper were an important purchase to flavour meat preserved by salting.

The church of **St. Cross** was built in the late 19th century, like many others in this area. Beside it stands the celebrated **Thorn Tree**. The original one is said to have been an offshoot of the Glastonbury thorn, which is supposed to have grown from the staff of Joseph of Arimathea and to have bloomed at Christmas.

Appleton Thorn is the only place in England where the ancient custom of *Bawming the Thorn* is still continued. The word 'bawming' means 'adorning' and, in this case, the thorn tree is decorated with flowers, or ribbons, by children from the local school as they dance round it maypole fashion. As they dance, they sing a song composed long ago by Rowland Egerton Warburton, Lord of the Manor of nearby Arley Hall, to the tune of *Bonnie Dundee*.

> *Up with fresh garlands this midsummer morn,*
> *Up with red ribbons on Appleton Thorn.*
> *Come lasses and lads to the Thorn Tree today*
> *To bawm it and shout as ye bawm it, 'Hurray'!*

The ceremony takes place each June on Appleton Thorn Walking Day .

Another rhyme of his can be seen on the lintel of the *Thorn Inn*,

> *You may safely while sober sit under the Thorn*
> *But if drunk overnight it will prick you next morn.*

... A warning to revellers who over-indulge!

A PLACE TO VISIT

Arley Hall

Travelling south down the Arley Mile from Appleton Thorn brings you to the Arley estate, still occupied by descendants of the original family - the Warburtons. The present Victorian mansion was designed in Jacobean style by Rowland Egerton-Warburton, a colourful, talented character whose verses are evident on signposts around the area.

His artistic talents were passed down to his son who painted water colours, many of which can be found in the house. There is also some fine furniture and, in the grounds, services are still held in the private chapel designed by Anthony Salvin. Dating from the late 14th century, the cruck and timber tithe barn is probably the best in Cheshire and the adjoining stables have been converted into a cosy tearoom.

Other attractions include: a gift and plant shop, craft workshops and tractor rides to visit Stockley Farm. Here, children are encouraged to touch the animals, feed calves and lambs, and tumble about in the straw. Nearby on the green stands the old school with timbered walls and tiny bell tower.

The gardens are impressive. A herbaceous border, dating from 1846, is thought to be one of the earliest established in England, and the avenue of cylindrical ilex is the only one of its kind anywhere. Also to be enjoyed are: an attractive avenue of pleached limes, banks of azaleas and rhododendrons, gardens of roses and herbs, a scented garden, a vinery, a wide, furlong walkway, and several secluded woodland walks.

Arley Hall and Gardens are open every afternoon except Mondays, between April and October. Telephone: 0565 777 353.

St. Wildrid's Church, Grappenhall

AROUND GRAPPENHALL

Distance: 4 miles

Start: Grappenhall village (SJ 638 863)

By Car: From Junction 20 on the M6 take the A50 towards Warrington. Turn left into Bellhouse Lane after crossing the Bridgewater Canal. Continue through the village to the *Ram's Head* pub. Turn right here into a large car park.

Turn left down to the canal bridge past the church. Then turn right in a southerly direction down Australia Lane. You soon take the path to the right across fields to Broad Lane. Turn right, crossing the lane to a track on the left after 500 yards or so.

500 yards along this track it turns left to the corner of a field, where there is a stile to the right. Cross this stile and go to the left of the large water tank to another stile opposite. Climb this and cross the field to meet a path on the far side. Turn left and follow this path round to the right.

Keep right at the meeting of paths to join Lumb Brook Road. Turn right along the road and keep right past houses, staying on the road to the canal aqueduct. Go under this and immediately turn right up a steep path to the canal. Then follow the towpath back to Grappenhall.

Grappenhall village

A place of charm, with cobbles, stocks - still in use last century, and a sandstone wall round an estate once the Greenall family home. The *Parr Arms*, named after a well known local family, has a coat-of-arms over the door, while the *Ram's Head* boasts an old sundial on the wall.

Built of sandstone from a local quarry, **St. Wilfrid's church** has many interesting features, including a medieval, stained glass window. The black cat sprawled along the tower's outside wall is said to have been Lewis Carroll's inspiration for the Cheshire Cat. The church's ironwork was made in the local smithy by George Fairhurst, the village blacksmith, and a grave marked with a skull and cross-bones is that of a plague victim.

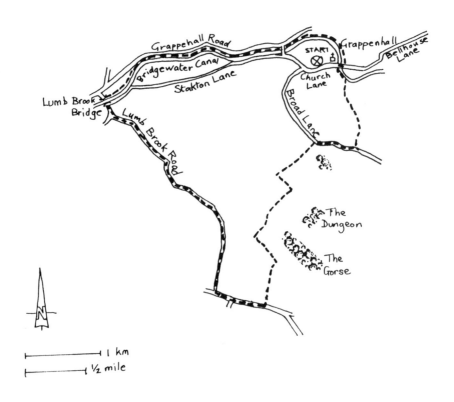

Grappehall Road

Bridgewater Canal

Stakton Lane

START

Grappenhall

Bellhouse Lane

Church Lane

Lumb Brook Bridge

Lumb Brook Road

Broad Lane

The Dungeon

The Gorse

N

1 km

½ mile

Around Grappenhall

AROUND LYMM

Distance: 4 miles

Start: The car park outside the church hall (behind Lymm Church).
(SJ 684 867)

By Car: Take the A56 east from Warrington to Lymm. After Lymm
Dam turn right up Crouchley Lane. Parking is on the right.

Follow the path to the right of the bridleway. After passing the Ranger's
cabin go along the outside of the avenue of Lombardy poplars to
Crosfields Bridge. The best view of this occurs as you turn left after the
bridge into the woodland known as *Lymm Bongs*.

Crosfields Bridge

Follow the stream edge and then continue between two layered thorn
hedges. (You can also walk in the woodlands to the left where the Mersey
Valley Partnership manages the public access with the landowner's
permission.) All the footpaths converge to cross Bradley Brook, where
the stepping stones which replaced Scholars' Bridge have now, in their
turn, been replaced by a board walk.

After crossing the brook keep to the path up steps between a modern
plantation of softwoods (larch and pine) and traditional English
hardwoods. Cross a stile and follow the left-hand side of the field to the
next stile, which takes you onto a farm track. Continue past the next gate
to a stile on the right. Enter the field here and follow the edge, as indicated
by the signpost, through to Knutsford Road.

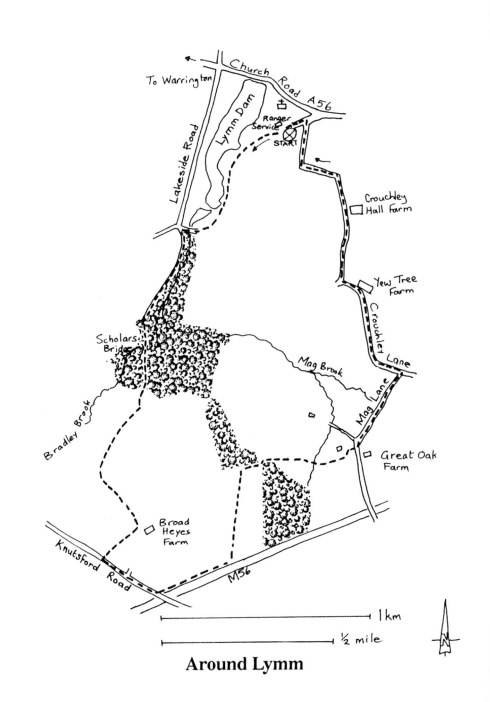

Around Lymm

Turn left past Primrose Hill Nurseries and the entrance to Broadhays Farm. Just before the motorway bridge turn left again over the stile leading into a farm lane. Climb over the stile at the end and follow the right hand side of the field by the motorway, turning left at the corner by the wood.

Continue along this field edge until a stile on the right leads you into the wood. Go through the corner of the wood coming out again over a stile. Walk across the middle of the field towards the farm to the left of the motorway bridge. Go over the ditch by the two ladder stiles, then head slightly to the left of farm buildings, towards the corner of the hedge.

Now follow the hedge on the left to a stile which leads onto Mag Lane. Turn left, and left again at the junction with Crouchley Lane, passing Yew Tree Farm and Crouchley Hall Farm to reach your starting point.

St Mary's Church, Lymm

Much painted, Lymm church stands on the most picturesque of sites. Inside, a handsome stone reredos has five panels intricately carved with scenes from Christ's passion, and several memorial windows are dedicated to local families. The tower has a ring of eight bells, the tenor being the second heaviest in Cheshire, beaten only by the one at Chester cathedral.

Wildlife on Lymm Dam

Lymm Dam once powered a mill for slitting steel but today provides a home for ducks and wildfowl. Most common are mallards but other darker birds may be coots or tufted ducks. Red-billed moorhens are more shy, often hiding in the undergrowth around the edge of the lake.

Also look out for the rarer great-crested grebe, which performs a fascinating courtship display, then carries its young chicks on its back.

great crested grebe

Ponds were once common in the countryside but have been lost as the reasons for their existence have disappeared: marl pits, drinking water for cattle, steam engine troughs. The conservation of remaining ponds is very important for the wildlife which depends on these habitats, and three ponds have recently been restored in *The Bongs*.

Many of our woodlands are desperately in need of conservation management; they are overgrown with no new saplings to replace mature trees when they die. Shading by rhododendron or sycamore (both invasive foreign species) also prevents woodland flowers, such as bluebell, primrose and lesser celandine, from thriving. A programme of felling, thinning and replanting to secure a future for the local woods is also being carried out in *The Bongs*.

AROUND OUGHTRINGTON

Distance: 4.5 miles

Start: Lymm Cross (SJ 684 872)

By Car: Take the A56 east from Warrington. At Lymm turn left onto the A6144. Turn into Pepper Street at Lymm Cross, where there is parking.

From Lymm Cross walk up Pepper Street to the school. Go straight ahead where Pepper Street leads to a bridleway to Oughtrington Lane. Turn left along this and cross the canal via Lloyd's Bridge, going down to the towpath and walking away from Lymm, with the canal on your right.

Go under the next bridge, Granthams, and over the aqueduct at Burford Lane. Pass the old mill (now the Vincent Owners Motorcycle Club spares depot), the Wharfage Boat Company (its holiday boats painted in traditional colours), and Hesford Marine, which still makes boats.

Shortly after Lymm Marina, leave the towpath at Agden Bridge, walking over the bridge to start your homeward journey. Turn right onto Warrington Lane. After 500 yards turn left at the footpath sign, following the footpath to the right of a hedge.

At the corner turn right but stay in the same field. At the hedge's end go through a gap and turn left. Walk to the top of this field with the hedge on your left, then stay in the same field, turning right at the corner. At the field's end go straight ahead over four stiles with yellow arrows, keeping the hedge on your left until you reach Burford Lane.

Turn right for about fifty yards, then go left over a marked stile into a field. At the field's end is Helsdale Wood, with flooded Helsdale Quarry immediately in front of you. Turn right following the edge of the trees to the waymarked stile, which takes you into the wood.

Follow the path straight through the wood, and between rhododendrons, to a stile. Cross the stile and follow the left-hand side of the field to Oughtrington Lane, close to the church. Turn left, walk past the church

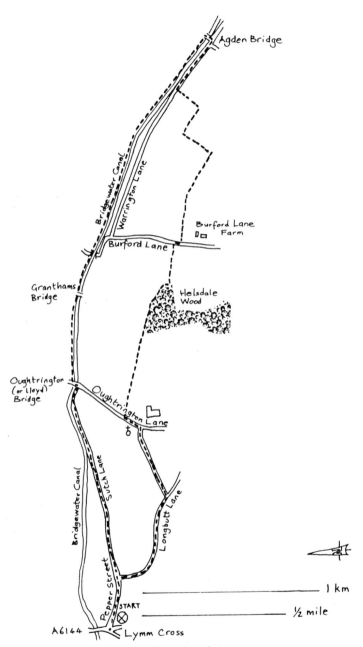

Agden Bridge

Bridgewater Canal

Warrington Lane

Burford Lane Farm

Burford Lane

Granthams Bridge

Helsdale Wood

Oughtrington (or Lloyd) Bridge

Oughtrington Lane

Bridgewater Canal

Sutch Lane

Longbutt Lane

Pepper Street

1 km

½ mile

START

A6144

Lymm Cross

Around Oughtrington

and turn right onto the marked footpath. This comes out onto Longbutt Lane, where you turn right back to Pepper Street.

Names

Most place names around here are English, showing that the area was settled by the Saxons. An exception, however, is Helsdale, the name for both wood and quarry. This is a Norse name but may be newer, borrowed from somewhere else.

Some names refer to people: Oughtrington was from the farmstead of the family of Oughtere. More recently, **Lloyds Bridge** was named after a local family who worked on the Bridgewater Canal for 200 years. It was previously called Dog Bridge because the *Dog Inn* stood nearby. A row of fustian cutters' cottages can still be seen from the bridge although the top storey, where the work was done, has since been removed.

Pepper Street is a name often found near a market cross, a place where spices could be bought - so important to flavouring a diet of stale, salted meat in medieval, and even much later, times.

Lymm Cross is one of the best examples of a village cross still in existence, although its exact age is unknown. In past times it was used as a preaching cross, not least by the Primitive Methodists who could always be sure of a good audience on Rushbearing Sundays.

Lymm Cross

The Bridgewater Canal originates from the second half of the 18th century, when the Duke of Bridgewater revolutionised transport from Manchester to the sea by cutting a canal to Runcorn. Today, this survives as a pleasure waterway and the towpath is an attractive route from Lymm's centre to the surrounding countryside.

St. Peter's Church, Oughtrington, is a fine example of Victorian Gothic architecture. The stone for its structure came from nearby Helsdale Quarry and its tall spire soars into the sky, a prominent local landmark.

George Dewhurst, a local cotton manufacturer, provided money for the church and the children of the family paid for the organ. All the woodwork is of oak except for the pews, which are of deal - cotton having hit a bad patch when these were made. The magnificent chancel is an exact replica of the one at Westminster Abbey and, in the glorious, stained glass, east window, designed by Kempe, a wheatsheaf is hidden - his trademark.

AROUND STOCKTON HEATH

Distance: 6.5 miles

Start: Mitchell Street, near London Bridge (SJ 615 858)

By Car: Take the A49 from Warrington and, after passing through Stockton Heath, turn right down Mitchell Street just before London Bridge. Park anywhere in this area.

Start near London Bridge, on the canal side near the boat shop on Mitchell Street. Follow the towpath under the bridge for nearly half-a-mile to the aqueduct over Lumb Brook Road. Just after the aqueduct a steep path to the left takes you down to the road. Go under the bridge and cross the road, following the brook to Bridge Lane.

Keep following the brook on your left, entering Appleton Dingle. The Dingle footpath will lead you through the woods to Dingle Lane. Turn left, cross the road and enter a second wood, Ford's Rough, by a gap on the right. This path takes you to Dood's Lane.

Cross to the track between hedges opposite. After 500 yards go over the waymarked stile on the right and follow waymarks over four more stiles to Cann Lane. Turn left and then right at the road junction. Follow the road to Stretton Church and turn right immediately after the churchyard wall. This path will bring you to a roundabout on London Road.

Cross London Road and walk down Hillside Road opposite. Follow this road, bearing right to Hillside Farm. Keep right at the farm where a stile lets you onto a track, which you now follow for nearly a mile. To your right is the highest part of Hill Cliffe, marked by a stone obelisk with four lions at its base.

After passing Bellfield Farm turn left along Firs Lane. Take the signposted path to the right just before Daintith's Farm. Bearing left, this path leads you across the golf course to Hough Lane, where you turn right. Cross the canal bridge, then turn right along the towpath back to the start.

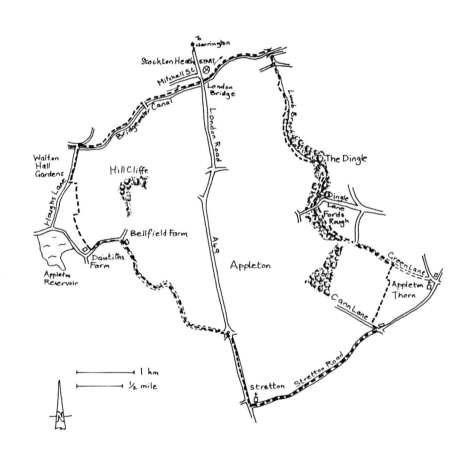

To Warrington

Stockton Heath START
Mitchell St
London Bridge

Bridgewater Canal

London Road

Lumb Brook

The Dingle

Walton Hall Gardens

Hill Cliffe

Dingle Lane
Fords Rough

Haughs Lane

Bellfield Farm

Daintiths Farm

A49

Appleton

Green Lane

Appleton Thorn

Appleton Reservoir

Cann Lane

1 km

½ mile

N

Stretton

Stretton Road

Around Stockton Heath

Around Stockton Heath

On completion of the Bridgewater Canal late in the 18th century, the London Bridge area, bustling with freight and passengers, was known as **Stockton Quay.**

Stockton House was the home of the agent in charge of the wharf, while the building adjoining the *London Bridge* pub was the village smithy. The rounded flight of steps in front of the pub was used by people embarking on the packet boat to Manchester at a fare of 1d per mile.

Lumb Brook Bridge is an aqueduct built to carry the Bridgewater Canal over Witherwin Lane (now Lumb Brook Road). Designed by the famous engineer, James Brindley, it was completed in 1770 and has a datestone on the north face.

Lumb Brook Bridge

In a book of prose published in 1773, John Aikin of Warrington Academy wrote an allegory unfavourably comparing the canal with the stream. The nearby Cobbs housing estate is built on the site of an old quarry and the word *cobb* means a round lump.

Until the 1930s, Lumb Brook fed a water mill and pond on the north side of Mill Lane, Stockton Heath. Eels bred in the water and skating was popular in Winter. The mill had a variety of names through the years: Bates Mill in 1770, Latchford Mill in 1877 (when there were brickfields to the west), Blinston's Mill in 1929.

Lumb Brook Valley

Over one mile in length, Lumb Brook Valley (*Lumm* meaning a deep hole) has all the features of a major valley in miniature. It is first mentioned in a Charter at the end of the 12th century, when it was given to Adam de Dutton at a rent of 12d (5p) per annum.

The ownership remained with the same family until the 1840s when it was divided between local landowners: Egerton Warburton of Arley Hall, Thomas Lyon of Appleton Hall and Thomas Parr of Grappenhall Heyes. And so it remained until 1939. During this time, the steep-sided valley was surrounded by meadowland and pasture, and crops of wheat, potatoes, turnips, mangel-wurzels and oats were grown.

The valley itself is divided into two sections by Dingle Lane (*Dingle* also meaning a deep hollow). The north end is known locally as **The Dingle** and is much used by local people. Its slopes are mainly covered by sycamore and oak, plus one bank of mature beech and some larch, pine and hornbeam. Flowers such as lords and ladies, wood anemone, campion and bluebell adorn the grassy slopes, and there are thickets of bramble and rhododendron.

red campion and bluebell

Ford's Rough, the narrower, steeper, southern section, is more secluded and has pretty clumps of primrose and bluebell in Spring. Here, outside bend erosion and inside bend deposition are very evident in the stream's incised meanders, and tiny waterfalls burble in the valley bottom.

The valley ends at Doods Lane (perhaps derivating from the word *dowd* meaning dull, lifeless, stale). From this point the stream becomes Dipping Brook and meanders under Cann Lane. Its name may originate from *canne* (a cup), perhaps referring to a ladle placed by a local well.

St Matthew's Church, Stretton

The church at Stretton was built in 1826/7 to the design of the eminent architect, Gilbert Scott. A new nave and tower were added later in that century in memory of the Vicar, Richard Greenall. He, and Thomas Lyon, were mainly responsible for the building of the church school (now a private house) in 1838.

From the top of the square tower seven counties can be seen on a clear day and the ring of six bells call parishioners to worship each Sunday. Nearby stands the tiny church hall, built by Colonel Lyon of Appleton Hall as a stable for his horse while he attended church.

The unusual clock faces on the tower have letters instead of numbers. One reads: TIME IS NOT ALL, the other, FORGET NOT GOD, and it is one of only three in the country where the figures have been replaced.

The stained glass, east window of the church depicts the Ascension of Christ and was given by parishioners in memory of Canon Charles Cross, a much loved man who was both frugal in habit and generous in nature. He was Vicar here for 40 years and is still remembered with great affection by older members of the congregation.

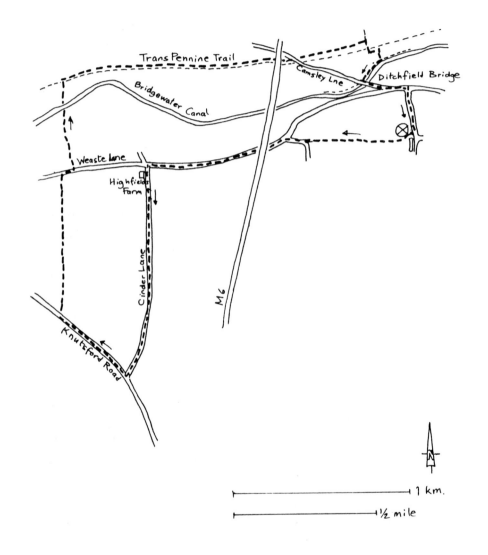

Around Thelwall

AROUND THELWALL

Distance: 4.5 miles

Start: Highfield Road, opposite its junction with Hardy Road. (SJ 673 868)

By Car: Take the A56 east from Warrington to Lymm. After passing under the M6 take the second right turn into Highfield Road. Park either here or in Hardy Road.

Follow the footpath sign which takes you down a narrow snicket between high hedges, then into a field. Keep ahead at a signpost, after which the path may be muddy.

At Booth's Lane bear right to Massey Brook Lane, where you turn left under the motorway, then pass Massey Brook Farm and Thelwall Grange. At Highfields Farm, and the junction of Massey Brook Lane, Weaste Lane and Halfacre Lane, turn left down the bridleway known as Cinder Lane.

Turn right along the A50 (Knutsford Road). Pass kennels then turn right at a footpath sign. This takes you alongside fields, then through a snicket between houses to Weaste Lane. Turn right here and immediately left , crossing a field to Pickering's Bridge and the Bridgewater Canal.

Keep ahead here to drop down onto the Trans-Pennine Trail at the bridge over the defunct Warrington-Altrincham rail link. Turn right and, after walking under the M6, leave the track at the next footbridge. Cross this and keep along a footpath, which bends left in front of picturesque cottages, then right to the Bridgewater Canal.

Turn right here and walk up a cobbled track at the next bridge to turn left along the A56 for a short way. Cross this busy road with care and take the second right turn up Highfield Road and back to the start.

Names

Some place names are descriptive such as Weaste for waste land and the later Cinder Lane. However, Pickering Bridge, Pickering Crescent and the *Pickering Arms* are all named after a Lord of the Manor who settled here in 1662.

AROUND RUNCORN

Aston	Keckwick
Daresbury	Moore
Halton	Runcorn Hill
Hatton	

Maps

The relevant maps for these seven walks are Warrington (SJ 68/78), Widnes (SJ 48/58) and Ellesmere Port (East) (SJ 47/57).

Local Landscape

Red sandstone dominates here, with outcrops to the south of the river valley, particularly at Keckwick, Runcorn, and Halton where the ruins remain of the Norman castle, once prominent on the skyline. The lower land of the Mersey valley is wetter, often flooded after rain, and would have been washed by high tides in the past.

Quarrying

The sandstone here dates from the Triassic period, 230 million years ago. Patterns in the rock show how the sand was built up in the dunes and water channels of a hot river delta, and the mineral, mica, gives the stone an attractive sparkle. Extensive quarrying took place in this area, the stone being very popular for churches and public buildings in the 19th century. Runcorn had the biggest quarries, supplying material for both Chester and Liverpool Anglican cathedrals, and even for part of New York harbour.

Farming

Mineral-rich clay from Ice Age glaciers on top of well-drained sandstone has led to good agricultural land, traditionally kept as pasture for dairy cattle. However, the second half of the 20th century has seen a swing towards corn production, with crops such as rape, with its bright yellow flowers, grown for the oil from its seeds. This trend may now reverse as livestock production becomes a more cost-effective way of using land, or new crops may become predominant.

Woodlands

In this area many more trees may soon be planted for their timber, as they grow well here. At one time, Delamere Forest extended as far as the Mersey marshes. Many small woodlands survive, often due to the popularity of pheasant shooting during the past 150 years, the trees providing good cover for the game birds.

Herons, majestic in flight, may be seen in the Weaver valley.

AROUND ASTON

Distance: 5.5 miles

Start: Aston Church (SJ 556 785)

By Car: Leave the M56 at Junction 11 and take the Northwich road (A56) through Preston Brook. Turn left at the first roundabout, then right at the next down Aston Lane South. Continue to Aston and park on the straight stretch of road near the church.

Look into St. Peter's churchyard to see the octagonal bowl of the 17th century stone font, then go through the kissing gate opposite the war memorial and bear right along the hedge. Continue through a gate and keep in the same direction to the road. Turn left and immediately right to Birdswood Farm.

Keep directly ahead at the farm buildings, walking through the cow byre (and mire!), then alongside a shed and through right-hand gates, which take you onto a cart-track. Keep ahead until you climb over a stile at the corner of Birds Wood.

The walk through this magical wood may be difficult in Summer because of the bracken. The path, even in Winter, is indistinct at first but keep ahead, then bear left through a clearing. The way then gradually becomes easier to follow, taking you down through the wood, across a stream and up the other side of the valley, where it broadens out for a while.

From here bear right to the wood's corner and follow a hedge and fence to a farm track. Then turn left over a stile and keep on the bridleway along a hedge. This winds down over the next field to a railway underpass.

Keep ahead again to pass the end of Longacre Wood, then ascend to walk between the buildings of Dutton Lodge Farm. At the junction ahead turn right down a private road, passing a wood and the road leading to Island Farm on the left, then crossing a stream.

At the far side of a thicket here turn left off the farm road and stride out over the field (keeping the stream on your left) to a sturdy, steel gate in

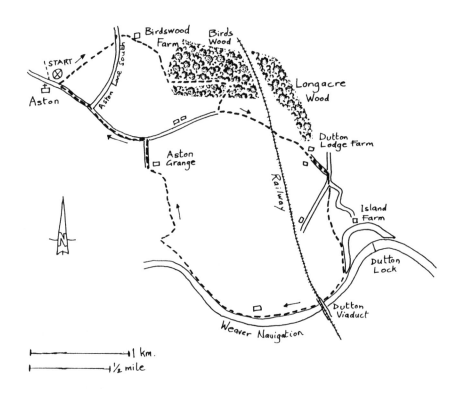

Birdswood
Farm

Birds
Wood

START

Aston Lane South

Longacre
Wood

Aston

Aston
Grange

Dutton
Lodge Farm

Railway

Island
Farm

Dutton
Lock

N

Dutton
Viaduct

Weaver Navigation

1 km.
½ mile

Around Aston

the fence. Go through this and keep in the same direction, following the stream down to the old course of the River Weaver, which leads to the recently renovated white bridge.

Turn right along the Weaver Navigation, once abustle with traffic, and walk under the massive, many-arched Dutton Viaduct, through another steel gate and along Pickering's Cut. Long-horned cows may herald your approach. Pass a picturesque Cheshire cottage, still sporting its original diamond-paned windows.

Go through another steel gate and on alongside the tranquil water, with birds a-twitter in the hawthorn. After the next gate veer right across the field ahead to hit a track at the wood's corner. Keep right along this and continue past Acton Grange and then along an unclassified road. Turn left at its end, crossing over the road to walk along the footpath back to the church.

Dutton Locks
The River Weaver was considerably straightened here to facilitate salt traffic, then later, ocean-going vessels from ICI at Winnington. Nowadays, however, it is mainly used by pleasure boats.

Dutton Viaduct
Completed in 1836, this carries the Chester to Manchester railway line over the River Dane and the Weaver Navigation. Comprising 22 stone arches and two wrought iron girder bridges, it was one of the most successful and safe engineering feats of its time. There were no accidents to the workforce during construction, many of whom were Irish and lived in the terraced cottages at Pickering's Wharf.

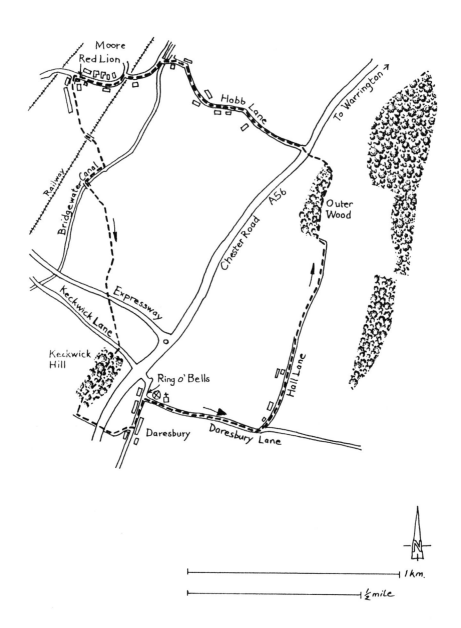

Around Daresbury

AROUND DARESBURY

Distance: 3.5 miles

Start: Ring o'Bells in Daresbury village (SJ 579 829)

By Car: Take the A56 from Warrington. Approaching Daresbury, keep ahead at the roundabout, then turn left into the village and right into the pub car park. (Groups should check with the landlord.)

Walk down Daresbury Lane, opposite the Ring o'Bells. Just after the entrance to Daresbury Hall turn left down Hall Lane, walking along this track until it ends in a field. Keep to the field's edge, following waymarks to Outer Wood.

Keep along the edge of the wood until you turn left at the end down a track. Cross Chester Road again to sandstone-lined Hobb Lane, which drops down to Moore village. Cross Moore Bridge and turn left along the canal towpath.

A few yards further on a tramp's gravestone lies beneath the wall - sometimes decked with posies of wild flowers. Cross the canal at the next bridge (on the track to New Manor Farm), then immediately turn right over the stile into a field. Follow waymarks to the next field and cross this to steps up to the Expressway.

With great care cross this main road and go down steps into the next field. Walk over this field to Keckwick Lane. On the opposite side of the lane is an entrance and steps, which lead into the woodland of Keckwick Hill. Walk through the wood to the opposite (south) side and turn left over a stile towards Daresbury.

At the far side of the field another stile brings you to Chester Road. Again, take great care when crossing this main road. On the opposite side walk up steps, climb the stile into the field, then follow the hedge on the right into Daresbury village. Look for the Cheshire cat on the facing barn, then turn left down the village street back to the *Ring o'Bells*.

Daresbury and Lewis Carroll

Situated in lush farmland and on the old Roman road from Wilderspool to Chester, Daresbury was the village where Charles Lutwidge Dodgson, alias Lewis Carroll, spent his early years. Today, the village is full of memorials to him.

In a side chapel in All Saints church is the famous stained glass, memorial window, which features Carroll himself with Alice and many characters from the Alice stories, not least the White Rabbit, Mad Hatter, and the dormouse sitting in his teapot. His father would have preached from the exquisitely carved Jacobean pulpit and the boy, Charles, was baptised in the old stone font, now relegated to a place outside, near the lychgate.

Daresbury Church

The oldest part of the present church is the tower, which dates from 1550 and has an unusual rhyme telling the ringers how to conduct themselves - obviously an unruly lot in those days! This is also an acrostic - the initial letter of each line forming the word DARESBURY.

Across the fields stands **Daresbury Hall**, a fine Georgian mansion built in the 18th century by George Heron. It was his descendant, Rev. George Heron, a much respected Canon of Chester Cathedral, who baptised the infant Charles Lutwidge Dodgson in Daresbury Church in 1832.

The village school dates from 1600 and on its roof is an *Alice* weather vane made by the last village blacksmith in his forge further down the street - now *Duttons*. Cottage names reflect a bygone age: Coachman's Cottage, Cobbler's Cottage, Sexton's Cottage, the School House, the Old Post Office ... and look out for the Cheshire Cat on a barn's gable.

Adjoining the *Ring o'Bells*, once a coaching inn, is the courtroom where the local sessions were held each month until these were transferred to Stockton Heath in 1911. Today, this building and the adjacent barn are being converted into an exhibition centre where the author's life and works can be studied.

Ring o'Bells

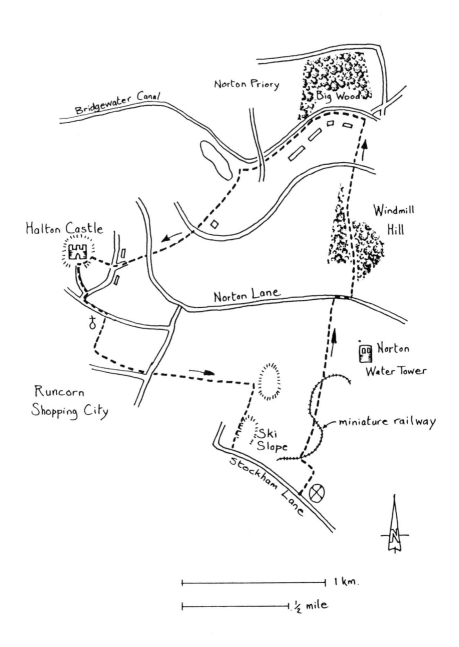

Norton Priory

Bridgewater Canal

Big Wood

Halton Castle

Windmill Hill

Norton Lane

Norton Water Tower

Runcorn Shopping City

miniature railway

Ski Slope

Stockham Lane

1 km.

½ mile

N

Around Halton

AROUND HALTON

Distance: 4 miles

Start: Stockham Lane (SJ 549 810)

By Car: From Warrington take the A56, turning right at the Daresbury roundabout onto the A558 Expressway towards Runcorn. Follow the M56 signs onto the A533 (Southern Expressway). Then follow Palacefields signs until the Town Park is also signed. From Greenhouse Farm Road turn right into Stockham Lane. Here, a small, secluded car park is on the left.

Turn right out of the car park, then left to cross the miniature railway track and pass a pond with dipping platforms. Stay on this path which follows the railway line, then a ditch, to Norton Lane. (Before reaching this, detour up the grassy hill for a closer inspection of Norton Water Tower.)

Turn right along the lane, then bear left at the hilltop and road junction into the wood on Windmill Hill. Carry on down the length of the wood, keeping parallel to the primary school's grounds before dropping down under two subways. Keep ahead again until you reach the Bridgewater Canal at Norton Townfield Bridge.

Turn left along the towpath here, which you may share with fishermen. On the opposite bank stretches Big Wood. At the end of this Green's Bridge affords a direct link with Norton Priory.

This walk, however, continues to the lake, where you turn left on the path away from the canal. Continue in the same direction, passing to the right of Woodlands Play Centre and on uphill, then under the subway and between purpose-built, concrete blocks of flats.

After the next subway veer right up steps, then continue uphill on this path until you climb steps in an old sandstone wall and walk along Mount Road. Cross the road at the far end with care and climb steps to the castle.

Walk around the castle walls to enjoy a panorama of outstanding views, stretching from Frodsham and Helsby Hills to the outstanding landmarks of Runcorn Bridge, Fiddlers Ferry, Daresbury Tower and Norton Water Tower. Below lies Runcorn's shopping city, convoluted road system, and a plethora of 20th century homes, both brick and concrete from many different decades, interspersed by the occasional sandstone gem from an earlier, less frantic era.

Leave the hill down Castle Road, passing the Boer War thanksgiving cross, St. Mary's church, the ancient library and old, weathered cottages. At The Underway turn right, cross the main road with care and turn left, then right down a path after Trinity Methodist Church.

Turn left before the subway and walk down to a roundabout. Cross Holt Lane at the traffic island here and take the path ahead, which immediately veers left into parkland. Take the second path to the right, passing the children's play area on your right.

Keep left where this path forks, take the second left at the next junction and turn right at the broader track ahead, which immediately crosses a stream. The bank ahead borders the arena - Runcorn's mini-Wembley! Turn right along the track here (or climb the bank to have a look).

This will take you back to the ski slope and your car. It is worth climbing up the back of the ski slope, for, on a clear day the summit affords rewarding views as far afield as Moel Famau and Kinderscout, Winter Hill and Mow Cop. It is also possible to pick out the route of the walk and the skiers often provide some entertainment.

Runcorn Town Park is by far the largest public open space in Runcorn. The dry ski slope is open throughout the year and refreshments are available. The miniature railway gets steam up most Sunday afternoons, providing a one-mile ride through the park.

Water Tower

Norton Water Tower was built in 1890, of red sandstone, and has been a dominant local landmark ever since. It was part of a scheme to supply Liverpool with water from Lake Vyrnwy in Wales, this being carried under the River Mersey by a tunnel 900 feet long and 10 feet wide. An oddity is that fish (presumably dropped by birds) bred in the water, so the top is now fenced off as a deterrent to both human poacher and heron!

Halton Castle

The castle ruins are over 900 years old, dating back to 1071 and the Norman settlement of England by William the Conqueror. Its excellent position atop a sandstone outcrop made it easy to defend, giving far-reaching views westerly to the hostile Welsh and easterly to the Pennine chain. It was used as a garrison for troops guarding the river crossings and as a hunting lodge for the wealthy barons.

Originally a motte and bailey of wood, in the 12th century it was rebuilt of stone, its foundations embedded in solid bedrock. Although soon to decline as a fortress, it remained as an administrative centre, court and prison, trying such petty crimes as theft, gambling and poaching fish from the then unpolluted Mersey. The Prior of Norton Priory was even brought to court there - for blocking the river passage - and, on a more serious note, two Welshmen who escaped from the cells in the 15th century were tried and hanged on the hill.

The Duchy of Lancaster inherited the castle in 1322 and still own it, although the pub belongs to Greenalls. In 1643-4, during the Civil War, the Royalist castle was besieged twice, and much of its structure was destroyed before it eventually fell to Cromwell's Roundheads, led by Colonel Henry Brooke of Norton Priory.

Some of the castle's outer defences still stand: towers in the fortifications, the archers' crossbow slits, the garderobe, and the sally porte with its fine roll-moulding. All the inner rooms were built into the walls and the only entrance was through the great gatehouse, where the court sat.

The gatehouse was pulled down in the 18th century and a new purpose-built courthouse took its place using the same stone - the *Castle Hotel* of today. The impressive Hanoverian coat-of-arms of King George III still decorates the doorway and court sittings continued until 1908. But as the lounge bar, the courtroom is now used by a different kind of customer!

St. Mary's church replaced an older building in 1820 but the stone vicarage dates back to the middle of the 17th century. The library dates from 1773 and its many ancient books are now being catalogued.

A PLACE TO VISIT

Norton Priory

Signposted from theA558 (Runcorn Expressway), this prize-winning modern museum is set in seven acres of beautiful gardens and is open every afternoon. Built on the site of the original Augustinian Priory, established in 1134, its treasures include: the 12th century undercroft, a mosaic floor, the finest Norman doorway in Cheshire, and a statue of St. Christopher - patron saint of travellers! The museum also has a large exhibition of medieval monastic life.

After the Dissolution of the Monasteries in the 16th century, the Brooke family lived here until 1921, in a Tudor, then a Georgian mansion, the last owner being Richard Brooke.

Close by is the recently restored Georgian walled garden, which includes a rose walk, herb garden, fruit and vegetable plots. The gardener's cottage and stables still exist too (the latter used as offices by the *Mersey Valley Partnership*). Many features from the Brooke estate can also still be seen, not only hedgerows, footpaths, crumbling walls and rhododendrons, but also summer houses and a stream glade.

Big Wood

A red shale path, bordered by alder, willow, ash and gorse, leads into the wood from the far end of the Norton Priory car park. Covering 23 acres, this wildlife refuge was once a deer park and hunting ground on the Brooke estate.

The path around the wood incorporates some attractive features from the original estate, including the old coach track, a Cheshire sandstone ha-ha on the western edge, and two bridges attractively faced in red sandstone. Although the wood consists mainly of oak and sycamore, there are specimens of many other trees, and rhododendrons line the canal bank.

The bird life is prolific. Pheasants still strut about and both green spotted woodpecker and sparrowhawk breed here. Bat boxes are also attached to the trees and foxes may silently slink through the undergrowth.

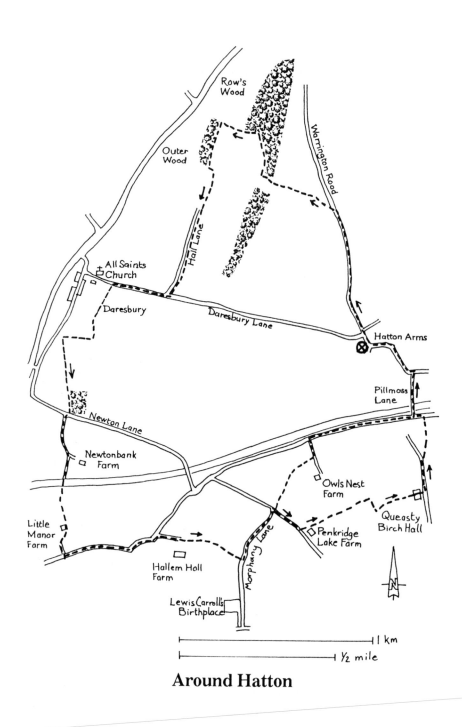

Around Hatton

AROUND HATTON

Distance: 6 miles

Start: *Hatton Arms* (SJ 599 824)

By Car: Take the A49 from Warrington. Turn right into Hatton Lane at Stretton traffic lights. At Hatton turn left into the large car park opposite the *Hatton Arms*. (The landlord asks that walkers should park at the far end, away from the pub.)

Turn left out of the car park, walking down Warrington Road to the second footpath on the left. Follow stiles and waymarks through Row's Wood to the corner of Outer Wood, then turn left along the edge of this wood to follow waymarks to Hall Lane.

Turn right at the end of this track down Daresbury Lane. Before the church turn left onto the footpath. Follow stiles and waymarks, turning right back towards the road. Do not leave the field but turn left again, aiming 50 yards to the left of the oak tree in the middle, then heading for the stile in the field's boundary.

Now follow stiles and waymarks again to Newton Lane. Take the track opposite towards Newton Bank Farm. Turn right before you reach the farm, following the footpath under the motorway and up the hill to Little Manor Farm.

Keep the red-roofed barn to your left and follow the farm track to Summer Lane, where you turn left. Then turn right down the track towards Hallem Hall Farm. Follow stiles and waymarks downhill to Morphany Lane.

(A detour to the right from here takes you to the site of the old parsonage - birthplace of Lewis Carroll. It has a commemorative plaque, information boards of his life and work, and is also a superb, if sometimes breezy, picnic spot.)

Retrace your steps and continue north-east to the junction with Newton Lane. Turn right here, then left at Penkridge Lake Farm. Turn left again beside the farmhouse, passing between cow byres, then turning right alongside the store of hay bales to a stile.

Keep ahead beside a barbed wire fence to the next stile, then straight ahead over the next field to two stiles separated by a bridge in the facing hedge. Walk ahead again across the next field, turning right on reaching the hedge to a stile. Turn left over this and follow the field boundary to Queasty Birch Hall.

Climb over the steel fence at the field's end, walking alongside the byre to a stile in the facing fence. Climb over two more stiles, then turn left along the cobbled farm track. Where the track bends left, keep ahead over (or round) a stile. Ascend a steep flight of steps and climb over a stile onto Summer Lane. Cross this with care and continue over the motorway on Pillmoss Lane. Turn left at the end of Pillmoss Lane back to Hatton.

Morphany Lane and the birthplace of Lewis Carroll

On 27th January 1832, Charles Lutwidge Dodgson was born at the old parsonage here. Son of the Vicar of Daresbury, he is better known today as Lewis Carroll, author of the *Alice* stories.

*from the memorial window
in Daresbury church*

The young Charles lived in this idyllic spot for the first eleven years of his life before his father moved to Croft, in Yorkshire. He went to Rugby school, then studied mathematics at Christ Church, Oxford, where he met Alice, the Dean's young daughter. The book *Alice in Wonderland* evolved from a story told to Alice on a picnic in July 1862.

The parsonage, which was also a working farm, was built on glebe land here, but was burned down in 1883. The site has recently been excavated and Lewis Carroll's birth is commemorated on a roadside plinth. The quote on it from one of his poems, *Three Sunsets*, refers to this very spot:

> *An island farm, midst seas of corn,*
> *Swayed by the wandering breath of morn,*
> *The happy spot where I was born ...*

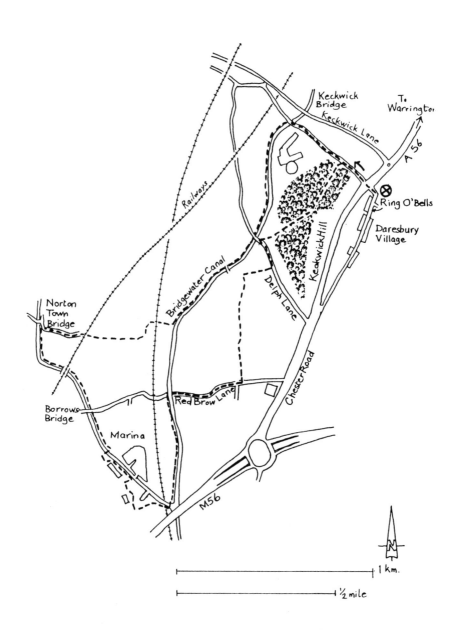

Around Keckwick

AROUND KECKWICK

Distance: 5 miles

Start: *Ring o'Bells* in Daresbury village (SJ 579 829)

By Car: Take the A56 from Warrington. Approaching Daresbury, keep ahead at the roundabout, then turn left into the village and right into the pub car park. (Groups should check with the landlord.)

Turn left out of the car park and walk to Chester Road. Cross with care and walk a little way down Keckwick Lane opposite. Turn left into a timber-lined entrance and up steps onto Keckwick Hill. You will soon arrive at a picnic site with excellent views of the surrounding countryside.

The large concrete tower is part of the nuclear physics research laboratory, opened by the prime minister, Harold Wilson, in 1967. The tower itself was built eight years later, much to the disgust of the locals.

Continue to the far end of the woodland, crossing a stile on your right into a young pine plantation known as the Daresbury Firs. Follow the path down the hill through the pines to Delph Lane, where you turn left. After a short distance turn right along the track to Crow's Nest Farm.

Before reaching the farmyard, turn left onto the marked permissive path and follow stiles and waymarks to Red Brow Lane. Turn right down the lane, which drops steeply through a gorge where mosses, liverworts, lichens and ferns cover damp walls. Pass under the aqueduct of the Bridgewater Canal and turn right up steps onto the canal towpath.

(Turning left here, back towards Keckwick Hill, would allow you to return by Delph Lane or Keckwick Lane to Daresbury village.)

For a longer walk, turn right at the top of the steps and follow the canal to a bridge near the motorway. Turn right across the old wharf here to Marina Village. Turn right again through the houses, then take the next right turn to the canal edge opposite the Marina.

From here turn left to cross the canal bridge. Turn left again back onto the towpath, which you follow towards Norton Bridge. Ten yards before the bridge turn right down a farm track. Pass under the railway, cross the site of Wharford Farm, walk under the next railway bridge and up to the canal again.

Turn left along the towpath here, past Daresbury Laboratory to Keckwick Lane Bridge. Walk up and over the bridge, up Keckwick Lane, across Chester Road, taking care again, to return to Daresbury village.

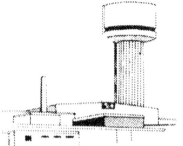

Daresbury nuclear physics laboratory

Keckwick

Despite its tiny size the ancient settlement at Keckwick is even mentioned in the Domesday Book. The plantation of firs on Keckwick Hill was cleared just after the 2nd World War, but was later replanted. The quarry there was largely filled in when the A56 was built.

AROUND MOORE

Distance: 5.5 miles

Start: Moore Nature Reserve (SJ 578 855)

By Car: Take the A56 from Warrington, turning right to Moore at the toast-rack bridge traffic lights. On approaching the village, turn right down Moore Lane, crossing two railway lines and the swing bridge over the Manchester Ship Canal. Parking is to the left off Lapwing Lane.

Walk back to the junction and keep ahead parallel with the railway, passing *Du Ponts* and other industrial works. To the left is aptly named Birch Wood, then some sand quarrying and a large lagoon. Turn right under the railway on reaching a road. Take a path to the left which is lined by willows and follows the River Mersey. Ascend steps, cross the A56 and turn right.

After the swing bridge over the Manchester Ship Canal, keep right on the A56, passing the *Ship Inn*. At the end of the next field turn left up the road to Walton Lea Nursery. George Crosfield (the local soap manufacturer) once lived in a mansion here. Keep ahead at cottages (built for the coachmen), round a gate, and ahead again to a further gate.

After this turn right, passing through a grassy gap, then turning left at the last poplar and crossing the field beside the strip of trees, to Walton Lea Road. Turn left here to Houghs Bridge, where you cut through railings and turn right under the bridge and along the towpath.

This is one of the prettiest stretches of the Bridgewater Canal. You may pass a line of fishermen, sitting in sombre reflection, before picturesque Walton Lea Bridge is reached. This leads into Walton Park with its many attractions.

You then pass St. John's church and the ancient cottages of Walton village, and maybe the sun will be glinting over Walton Bridge. Houseboats splash the opposite bank with vivid colour as you reach more open

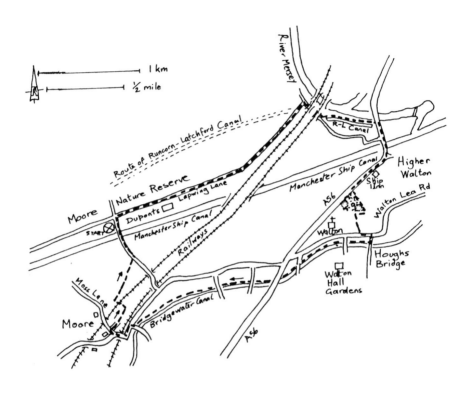

Around Moore

countryside. The canal passes under the toast-rack bridge, which carries the A56, and then over the now secluded, old Chester Road. Thomason's Bridge is next, then Acton Grange Bridge, before the outskirts of the village and Moore Bridge are reached.

Leave the canal here and turn left along the road. Turn right down Moss Lane immediately after crossing the railway, then turn right again down rough Gigg Lane. Veer left over the railway, right alongside it, then left again through iron gateposts.

Turn right along the side of a field at the new bowling green. Keep in the same direction over several stiles; the last one, hidden in a corner, takes you onto Moore Lane. Turn left here where sand quarrying is still much in evidence. Cross the Ship Canal with its sturdy, brick tower and you are back at Moore Nature Reserve.

Moore Nature Reserve

A detour from the walk's starting point takes you on a fascinating Nature Trail. Lying between the Manchester Ship Canal and the River Mersey, Moore Nature Reserve was opened in 1992 as an oasis for wildlife. Yet the area has, for many years, been treasured by Warrington folk for its luscious blackberries.

Lying on the flight path of many migrating birds it is already a major focal point for ornithologists and several hides have been set up overlooking the lakes.

Over 100 different bird species have been counted and there are birds of prey such as kestrels and sparrowhawks.

The large islanded lake is a paradise for water fowl, including pochard, teal and tufted duck It also provides a nesting ground for both types of grebe. Nearby, lime-loving plants, including meadow cranesbill, survive on low-lying ground.

tufted duck

The heavily wooded Hawthorn Hill is renowned for long-eared owls; in fact every native species of owl except the barn owl breeds in the area. The wood is also rich in fungi and is particularly noted for the giant puffball.

The bed of the Runcorn to Latchford Canal runs through the Reserve. Only drained in 1976, the dressed stone of its containing walls can still be seen. Near it, stagnant ponds provide an ideal environment for toads, water violet, water dropwort and flag iris. Butterflies flit among harebells in rough meadowland - speckled wood, common blue and the rare clouded yellow.

himalayan balsam

Despite the nightmare of invasive Himalayan balsam, several different types of woodland are being developed. These include an oak wood, a birch plantation and an alder wood, where coppicing is taking place and loosestrife thrives.

Telephone UK Waste Management on 0925 444689 for more information.

Walton

Sir Gilbert Greenall, grandson of the founder of the local brewing firm, built Walton Hall as his family home. The cottages in the village were built for the estate workers, their sandstone facades cut and shaped at a stonemason's yard which stood by the hump-backed Walton Bridge.

The Walton Arms was originally called the Bay Horse Inn, and was also a farm which delivered milk twice daily to local households. George Duckworth, the England and Lancashire wicket keeper, was landlord there for a time.

The **Church of St. John the Evangelist**, Walton, with its cruciform shape, soaring, central spire 130 feet high, and idyllic setting, is almost a cathedral in miniature. It was built of Cheshire red sandstone late in the 19th century and was paid for by Sir Gilbert Greenall at a cost of some £17,000. The barrel-vaulted roof is magnificent, all the woodwork is richly carved (especially the reredos with its gospel figures), and there are some fine stained glass windows.

A PLACE TO VISIT
Walton Hall Gardens

This fine Victorian house, home of the Greenall family until 1941, is set in parkland and ornamental gardens, where rhododendrons and azaleas blaze with colour in late Spring. Other attractions are: a bowling green, children's zoo, adventure playground, miniature and crazy golf courses.

grey squirrel

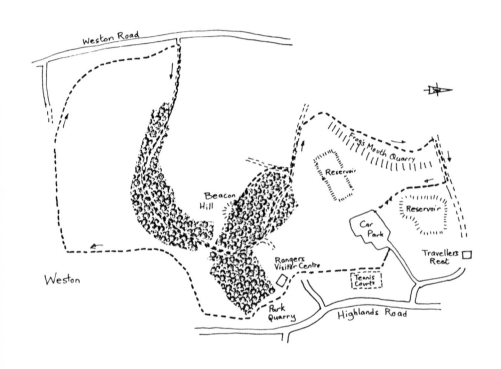

Weston Road

Beacon
Hill

Frog's Mouth Quarry

Reservoir

Reservoir

Weston

Car
Park

Travellers
Rest

Rangers
Visitor Centre

Tennis
Courts

Park
Quarry

Highlands Road

Around Runcorn Hill

AROUND RUNCORN HILL

Distance: 2.5 miles

Start: The car park on Runcorn Hill (SJ 508 819)

By Car: Travelling west, leave the A557 (Runcorn Expressway) at the sign for the Old Town. Turn immediately left onto Heath Road. After passing the impressive Town Hall, turn right at traffic lights down Moughland Lane. At the end turn left at the cenotaph, then immediately left again up Highlands Road at the post office. Turn right and left into the car park.

From 1734 until early this century Runcorn Hill was quarried extensively for much-prized red sandstone. Stone from here was used to build both Liverpool and Chester Anglican Cathedrals, Holker Hall and the great pillars of Tatton Hall, Peel Castle on the Isle of Man, and even part of New York harbour.

In the footsteps of the Quarrymen ...

Well signed with posts showing a blue hand and yellow arrow, this short walk is full of interest and exciting places for children to explore.

Walk back to the car park entrance and bear right down steps. Walk past tennis courts and bowling greens, then continue in front of the Ranger's cabin.

The earliest quarrying was carried out in Park Quarry here. It provided paving for Grappenhall village and stone for the Bridgewater Canal. Nearby stands a row of quarrymen's cottages. Early quarrying required brute strength as the only aids were crude hand tools and the most basic of hoists.

Keep ahead onto the footpath here, then cross the field to a seat, where you turn right down the slope, then ahead through the wood.

East Quarry here was once over sixty feet deep - the largest freestone quarry in Britain. Today it is but a shallow basin as, for many years, it was the town's rubbish dump.

Keep ahead along the fence.

The large open fields ahead were once gouged out by three quarries where the durable Weston red sandstone was found - so named after its colour and place of extraction.

Turning right at a stile follow another fence. Veer right before a gate, then turn left and keep ahead round the hill, where superb views stretch over the Mersey estuary to Hale lighthouse and beyond.

The bright pink cottage on Weston Road was once a quarryman's home. To its right is Orme's Cottage, where a quarry owner of that name once lived. The stone was always competitively priced as the quarry's own railway took it straight to Weston Point Docks to be loaded into lighters (flat cargo boats).

With new housing ahead, turn right under a footbridge and along a secluded walkway. Stay on this sheltered path - probably the oldest on the hill - until you eventually ascend sandstone steps. Keep ahead again then make a detour sharp left to the viewfinder. (To reach this quickly, bear left along a narrow path where the way forks.)

The viewfinder on Beacon Hill is the highest point of the area, where a beacon would have warned of invasion in earlier times. On a clear day, places as far apart as Snowdon and Shutlingsloe, Blackpool Tower and Biddulph Moor, can be seen, while below is the confluence of the River Weaver and the Mersey.

Retrace your steps to the reservoir and turn left through a cleft in the cliffs where the hinges of a huge gate can be seen - once the quarrymen's entrance. Turn right down steps into a valley and bear right along it.

Frog's Mouth Quarry takes its name from the shape of an outcrop here. The largest block of stone came from this quarry; it became the foundation stone for Liverpool's Anglican Cathedral.

The rock here was formed 200 million years ago; many fossils have been found in it and the footprints of several prehistoric creatures have given it the nickname, Valley of the Dinosaurs.

At the footpath at the far end turn right and you soon bear right again up a tiny path to another fine view. Far below is Weston Point Docks, the regular shipping place for the hill's sandstone.

From here either continue alongside the reservoir back to the car park or retrace your steps to the main path and turn right to the *Travellers Rest,* where you can slake your thirst as the quarrymen once did.

At Hale Cheshire's only lighthouse overlooks the Mersey estuary.

AROUND WIDNES

Hale Head Lighthouse	Pickerings Pasture
Hale Village	Spike Island
Pex Hill	

Map
The relevant map for these five walks is Widnes (SJ 48/58).

Local Landscape
The main feature of the area is the estuary of the River Mersey at its widest. Views stretch to the heights of Helsby and Frodsham, the industry of Ellesmere Port and beyond, and the Clwydian hills of Wales.

There were once extensive marshes by the river. Flooded at high tide, these were a feeding ground for ducks, geese and wildfowl. Few now remain as the growth of Widnes has required land for tipping. Until its recent transformation into a series of wildflower meadows, Pickerings Pasture was an active waste tip and, as a result of this, its site is now well above water level. Not long ago, however, it was a waterside meadow, with each high tide reaching Shore House at the park's entrance.

Although hardly used today, the river was once very important to shipping and Hale has the only surviving lighthouse on the upper Mersey. There is fertile farmland at Hale too, with a mixture of crops and, in the recent past, fields of daffodils and tulips were common. At low tide the river's sand and mud flats are exposed and there was once a route across the estuary to Runcorn, where pack horses and even carts daringly forded the channels.

Local Wildlife
The sand and mud are extremely productive as feeding grounds for birds, giving the estuary international significance as a home for ducks and waders. It is also classified as a Site of Special Scientific Interest by the Nature Conservancy Council. A decoy pool used to attract thousands of birds every year which were slaughtered for food. This is now a nature reserve managed by the Cheshire Conservation Trust.

Pickerings Pasture has a birdwatchers' hide and the clifftop paths bordering Hale also offer good vantage points for viewing the estuary's birdlife. Curlew, redshank and teal can be seen here in large numbers and you may also spot the larger shelduck. The shore also has a variety of wildflowers adapted to live in these extreme salt marsh conditions.

shelduck

HALE HEAD LIGHTHOUSE

Distance: 3 miles

Start: *Childe of Hale* pub (SJ 469 823)

By Car: Take Ditton Road west from Widnes, which goes to Hale village. The *Childe of Hale* faces you at the war memorial.

From the pub walk south down Church Road, away from the traffic island. After passing the old manor house on the left, turn left down Within Way. Follow this to its end and go through two pinch gaps, turning right after the second onto a path running parallel to the estuary.

Follow this footpath, which is part of the *Mersey Way*, between the edge of marsh and field, heading for the lighthouse. (There are two benches along this section where you can rest and enjoy the view.)

At the lighthouse pass through a pinch gap into the lane, where you turn right back to Hale village via Church Road. (Turn into the churchyard to visit the grave of the *Childe of Hale*.)

Local People

In the 16th century Hale had a giant - John Middleton. Nicknamed the *Childe of Hale*, he was nine feet three inches tall. Legend has it that he was very powerful and a notable wrestler, but he was a gentle giant. The thatched cottage where he lived can still be seen on Church Road and his huge grave survives in the churchyard. The Childe was a servant of the Lord of Hale.

The Blackburne family owned the estate until the 1930s when it was bought by the Heskeths. The hall no longer survives but the smaller manor house does and can be seen on the left near the beginning of both the Hale walks. The poet John Betjeman stayed there and wrote a poem entitled, *The Manor House, Hale, near Liverpool.*

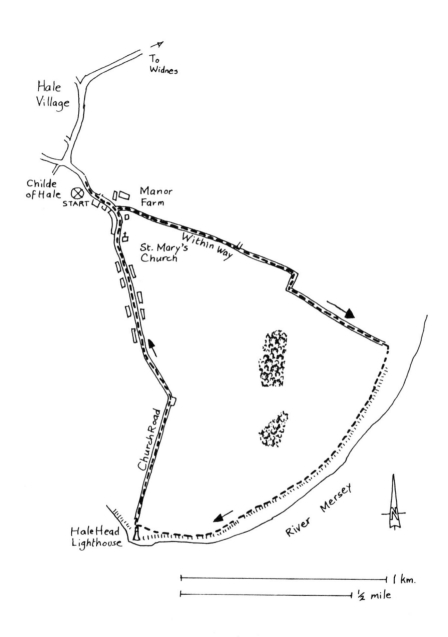

Around Hale Head Lighthouse

Around Hale

Hale Village dates back to Anglo Saxon times and, after the Norman Conquest, was sold to King John.

Hale lighthouse was built in 1906 and is the only lighthouse still standing in Cheshire. At a height of 45 feet the light was once visible for up to forty miles. It continued to be lit during the war and this probably resulted in several bombs falling nearby. The light was turned off permanently in 1958 and the building is now part of a private dwelling.

Cheshire's only lighthouse

The **Hale Duck Decoy** was used to lure ducks down its long, funnel-shaped waterways, where they were trapped and killed for the table. It is now a wildfowl refuge and Site of Special Scientific Interest.

A PLACE TO VISIT

Speke Hall

Owned by the National Trust, this stands to the west of Hale village, towards Liverpool. The Elizabethan manor house, built round a cobbled courtyard, is full of interest, with a great hall and smaller, panelled rooms with fine furnishings and priest holes. Outside are gardens and woodland, the drained moat and even an earth bank or *bund*.

Speke Hall is open every day between April and October, except Mondays. (Telephone: 051 427 7231)

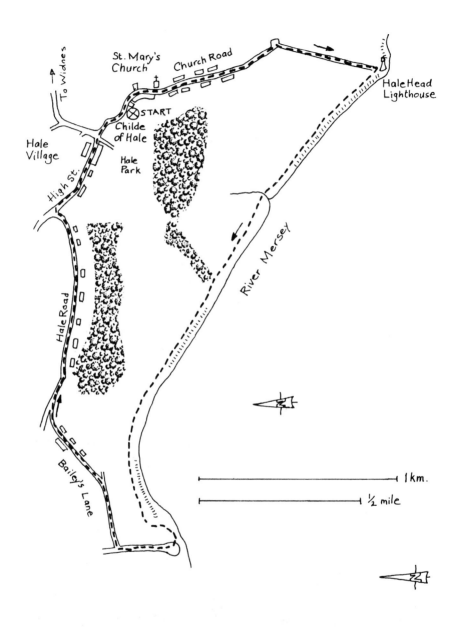

Around Hale Village

AROUND HALE VILLAGE

Distance: 4 miles

Start: *Childe of Hale* pub (SJ 469 823)

By Car: Take Ditton Road west from Widnes, which goes to Hale village. The *Childe of Hale* faces you at the war memorial.

From the pub turn south down Church Road, away from the traffic island. Follow the lane through the pinch gap by the gate, heading for the lighthouse. On reaching it turn right through another pinch gap, then follow this path along the clifftop. This is part of the *Mersey Way*.

Pass through a second gap and keep to the same path, crossing the brook by a small bridge. As you come to woodland keep following the path ahead, aiming for the lights of Liverpool Airport.

As you approach a privet hedge surrounding a large house take the flight of steps to the left down to a small bridge. Then walk up the opposite bank to a car park.

(From here you might decide to continue ahead along the *Mersey Way* for 3.5 miles to Garston foreshore.)

Otherwise, turn right here, following the lane away from the shore. After 200 yards turn right again into a second lane - just after the cottages but before the airport's landing lights.

Follow this surfaced road until it meets a wider road with bungalows opposite, where you turn right. This is Hale Road and from here it will take you about 15 minutes to walk back to the village centre.

Childe of Hale's cottage

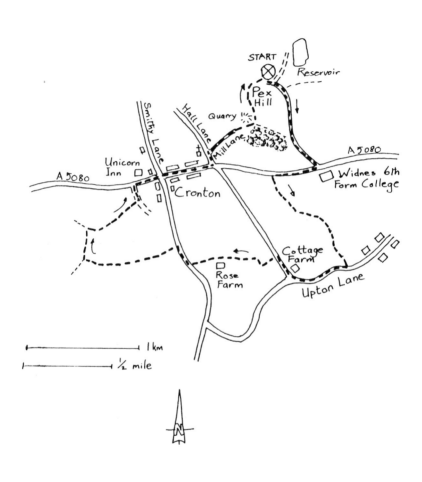

Around Pex Hill

AROUND PEX HILL

Distance: 3.5 miles

Start: Car park at the top of Pex Hill (SJ 501 888)

By Car: From Widnes take the A5080 west towards the M62. Turn right through green gateposts opposite Widnes 6th Form College. Continue up the hill to the car park.

Walk down the hill on the footpath parallel to the road, then continue down this to the A5080 which you cross and turn right. Turn left at the end of the first field along a footpath separating crops. Then cross a stream and continue ahead to turn right along Upton Lane.

From here views extend to the suspension bridge and the tall chimney, then from Halton's castle ruins, along the Overton Hills to Ince Power Station. Keep right at Cottage Farm with its huge barn, then turn left at the far end of a rough copse and follow the ditch along the field's edge. Keep ahead at Rose Farm to the road, where you turn right to pass Laburnum Cottage.

Turn left to cross the next extensive field on a clear path between crops. Keep in the same direction, crossing two deep ditches by plank bridges with handrails. Keep ahead again for a short way until you turn right at the far side of another ditch and walk along it. Turn right at the other side of the next dyke, walking beside this for a short distance until you turn left after crossing a further ditch. Meander along this dyke, turning left at the end along a muddy cart-track to the road.

Turn right here past the *Unicorn Inn* (est. 1752), Stocks Cottage with its glassy, mosaic walls, the war memorial and five-holed stocks. Keep ahead at traffic lights, where Smithy Lane turns left.

Pass the Black Horse, the Community Centre and Hillside Farm. Then turn left up Hall Lane and right up Mill Lane at the Roman Catholic church and the old school sign. Notice the ancient petrol pump and Mill Cottage, then continue ahead onto the hill.

Perhaps enjoy a scramble in the quarry with its rock climbing potential before bearing left at its far side up the hill. To explore the hill and enjoy the views, bear left again at the top end of the quarry, onto a path which meanders up the slope to the picnic tables and breezy view.

About Pex Hill

A superb vantage point, Pex Hill is an outcrop of triassic sandstone rising 200 feet about the Mersey Valley. It is the largest area of lowland heath in Merseyside, with wavy hair grass a notable plant, and an unusual stunted oak woodland on its lower slopes. Today, bracken is threatening to erase the heather but gorse, broom and bramble thickets provide nesting sites for birds such as yellow-hammer and linnet, while cuckoos are regular summer visitors and lizards sunbathe on exposed rocks.

Shaped flint pieces found on this hill indicate human activity during the Bronze Age - around 2,000BC. Uncertainty surrounds the name Pex (once Pecks and only changed in the mid-1800s). It may originate from 'pixie' or the name of an Anglo-Saxon landowner, or from *Pecks Mill* which once stood here.

The name **Cronton** means 'farmstead of Kroyenga' and there was a settlement there before 1066 when Pex Hill was common grazing land. Mill Lane, leading down to Cronton from the quarry, dates from the 13th century when there were probably two mills on the hill - a windmill and a horsemill.

As early as 1598 marl and stone were being dug from the hill on a small scale for building purposes, hence the crescent-shaped hollows which pit the surface. In 1698 Pex Hill House was built and its date stone lies in the reservoir wall.

Cronton Hall was built by Richard Wright in 1740 and is now used as a farmhouse. The ghost of Peg Pussy, a young farmer's daughter from Bold, is still reputed to haunt the hill. In 1787 she was supposedly lured to the hilltop by her lover, then thrown over the cliff and killed. Another tale is that, when spurned by her lover who slammed the door of Cronton Hall in her face, she went mad, rambling over the hill until she died.

The quarry, dating from the 19th century, provided building stone for the first two reservoirs, the earliest completed in 1869. Before the opening of the second, in August 1878, the contractor provided a lavish dinner inside it for workmen and guests. Marked by a booming cannon, its official opening ceremony in October was then attended by more than 3,000 people.

In 1939, a third reservoir, made of concrete, was built. In 1954 the first reservoir was demolished and five years later remedial repairs were carried out to the second. Walking up from the Visitors' Centre you can see its air vents to the left. The third reservoir lies under the earth mound on the right and they both supply water to the Widnes area.

An anti-aircraft battery was stationed here during the Second World War and the quarry walls are pock-marked with practice rounds. Later, a dance pavilion was a popular attraction, replaced today by an Observatory and Visitors Centre.

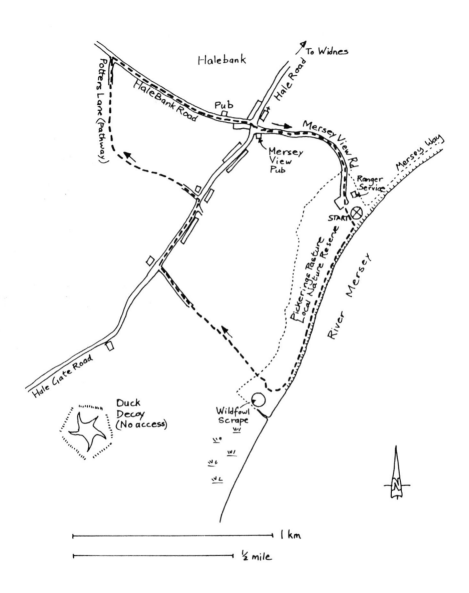

Around Pickerings Pasture

AROUND PICKERINGS PASTURE

Distance: 2.5 miles

Start: Pickerings Pasture car park (SJ 488 836)

By Car: Take Ditton Road west from Widnes. Cross over the railway before turning left at the *Mersey View* pub down Mersey View Road. Bear right and park overlooking the estuary.

From the car park near the Ranger's cabin pass through the gap in the low fence, following the path towards the river. Turn right and follow the path to the end of the site, turning right again near the blocks of limestone.

Continue on this path along the edge of trees and shrubs, perhaps making a detour to visit the bird hide; then walk up the slope and climb over the stile. Follow this path past the sewage treatment works and out onto Hale Gate Road.

Turn right along the road and, after 250 yards (after Garnetts Lane), cross the road with care to walk down the track opposite. The path follows an old lane between hedges and past brambles and shrubs, bending to the right after 200 yards.

Continue along this path to the road near the garage. Turn right at Hale Road, cross to Mersey View Road and follow this back to the start.

About Pickerings Pasture

Now a local nature reserve, Pickering's Pasture is a delightful surprise, its wildflower meadows giving wide views across the Mersey estuary. On the opposite shore Runcorn Hill rises behind the docks complex and the Overton Hills form an even higher backdrop. A brisk walk towards the elegant span of Runcorn Bridge takes you past an obelisk which replaced the original warning beacon used by shipping until 1971.

Ox-eye daisy

The flowers are manifold: daffodils in March, cowslips in April, ox-eye daisies in May. All herald the Summer glory of wildflower meadows awash with colour, when Yorkshire fog and sterile brome, cocksfoot, common vetch, common spotted orchid and purple loosestrife, all nestle among rough-stalked meadow grass. And then there's the cornfield in August, where corn cockle, poppies, corn chamomile, corn marigold and cornflower, all form a riot of colour among the wheat.

The many pink and blue flowers also attract numerous butterflies: peacock, orange tip, common blue, painted lady, small copper, small tortoiseshell, large skipper, large white and meadow brown - to name but a few. The six-spot burnet moth might also be seen, and white blooms attract other night-flying moths.

At the west end rough limestone blocks stand near a bird hide overlooking Hale Marshes. An RSPB reserve, these salt marshes are flooded by high tides and, until the 1950s, they covered the whole area and were grazed by cattle. Before recent reclamation, however, they had been used as a refuse tip.

An SSSI, the Mersey Estuary is one of Britain's most important winter feeding grounds for waterfowl. Redshank, curlew, teal, shelduck, wigeon, pintail and dunlin feed on the tidal mudbanks, sandbanks and salt marshes, while high overhead a peregrine falcon may patrol the sky.

AROUND SPIKE ISLAND

Distance: 2.5 miles

Start: The car park at the Catalyst Museum (SJ 514 842)

By Car: Follow Waterloo Road south from Widnes town centre. Turn left into Mersey Road, then go left again into the Catalyst Museum's car park.

In the footsteps of the Chemical Industry ...

At the car park entrance stands an enormous ceramic vat, once used to boil soda and slaked lime to make caustic soda.

(The MP, Jack Ashley, was born and bred on nearby West Bank.)

Walk down to the canal bank and turn right to the locks. Cross these and continue ahead, past the wet dock where swans may be overwintering.

One of the railway locks has been restored while the other has been converted into a slipway giving access from canal to river. Sparrowhawk and heron hover above the dock, which is also visited by red-necked grebe. Children enjoy feeding the resident swans and mallards. Facing the Mersey is the wooden rudder from a Mersey flat.

Across an open lawn to your left are two brickwork arches from the pyrite kilns of Hutchinson's vitriol works. Near them lie the massive stone bases of acid absorption towers. Sixty feet high, these were built of acid-proof Yorkshire flagstone.

At a canal bridge turn right along the towpath to the next bridge.

Ahead, vapour may be billowing into a blue sky from the cooling towers and tall chimney of Fiddler's Ferry Power Station.

(You may wish to continue further along the canal to explore the Fiddler's Ferry area and perhaps visit the *Ferry Inn.*)

If not, turn left across this bridge and, with care, cross the railway line. Continue ahead up Tan House Lane, passing *Zeneca*, a chemical firm

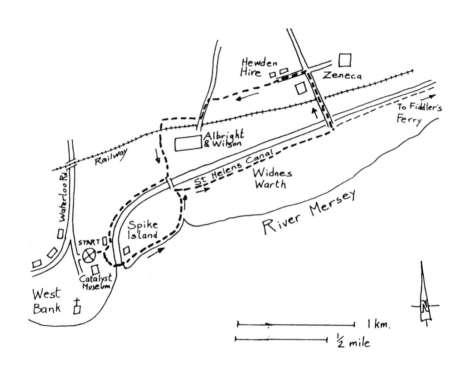

Around Spike Island

which makes Paraquat weedkiller. Immediately after crossing a single track railway turn left down Cornubia Road.

After passing a car dump, keep ahead down a litter-strewn footpath to the left of gates leading to *Hewden Hire*. Views extend over Runcorn Bridge to the Overton Hills as you cross grassland, then a raised bank, to reach a road.

Turn left for a short way towards the gates of *Albright & Wilson*. Then turn right down a tarmac footpath, which becomes muddy before it veers left under a railway and becomes worse! Keep left - a better surface is ahead! Continue forward to the canal bridge, walking on either side of the canal back to the starting point. Along here the yacht haven of West Bank Boat Club adds colour to the scene.

Point of Interest
Ideally, this walk should perhaps be combined with a picnic on *Spike Island* and a visit to the *Catalyst Museum*.

View from Spike Island across the River Mersey to Runcorn.

The History of Spike Island

Today, expansive views over the River Mersey and a network of paths have replaced the industry here, but it is still hard to imagine the area 150 years ago. Then it was a quiet riverside marsh grazed by sheep and cattle, where a rural farming community lived in a few tiny hamlets.

The first indication of industrial development came with the arrival of the St. Helens-Runcorn Gap railway in 1833, the same year that the Sankey Canal was extended to here. Both were built to transport St. Helens coal to the River Mersey.

At Spike Island, the first purpose-built railway dock in the world was constructed, to facilitate the transport of a huge annual tonnage of St. Helens' coal to Liverpool and Ireland. Built side-by-side, twin locks enabled two boats to enter or leave at the same time. In those days Spike Island was covered with railway sidings, and a reservoir provided water for a wet dock, entered from the River Mersey.

In 1849, Spike Island also became the birthplace of the British Chemical Industry, when John Hutchinson built his alkali works here. These were soon followed by William Gossage's soap works in 1854.

Widnes was ideally placed for these alkali works, which produced salt-cake and soda for textiles, glass and soap manufacture until the end of the 19th century. Coal was mined at St. Helens, Irish labour was cheap following the potato famine of 1845-7, limestone, salt and metal ores were easily imported.

So Widnes was suddenly transformed from a sleepy village with a population of only 2,000 in 1840 to a town of 15,000 in 1870. Hutchinson's chemicals and Gossamer's soapworks continuously belched forth smelly gases and clouds of black soot, so that the area was almost permanently covered by a huge pall of smoke.

Many of the back-to-back, terraced streets in Widnes were hastily constructed during this time. 'Spikes' were the cheap lodging houses for chemical workers operating a twelve hour shift - the beds never cold!

Working conditions in Hutchinson's alkali works were both dangerous and unhealthy: hydrogen chloride rotted teeth; unhealthy fumes clogged lungs; chlorine irritated eyes. The workers' main recreation was going to the pub. No trees grew in Widnes at that time.

Before the end of the 19th century, Gossamer's Works was the largest soap works in the world. With 900 employees in 1897, it produced half of England's soap products. It was also the first soap company to use brand names and develop 'marbled' soap and, in his research laboratory, Gossage devised uses for waste products. Soon however, Gossage's was bought by William Lever of Port Sunlight, the brand names changed to *Lifebuoy* and *Sunlight*, and the works were eventually closed by Unilever in 1932.

In fact, by the beginning of the 20th century, with huge improvements in technology, plus new works at Winnington and Weston Point (Runcorn), and deep-water docks at West Bank, industry had moved away from Spike Island. Hutchinson's Works closed in 1919 but this was not before both Ludwig Mond and Brunner (co-founders of ICI) had served their apprenticeship in their laboratories. The dock was closed in 1925, replaced by deep water access to the River Mersey at West Bank, Garston and Runcorn, and by the Manchester Ship Canal.

From the 1930s to the '70s the area was a derelict eyesore encompassing disused factories, piles of waste and an abandoned canal. Despite the danger of crumbling buildings and chemical waste, generations of Widnes children used the site as an adventure playground.

The pyrite furnaces, partially buried under dumped waste, offered the excitement of caves. The youngsters even swam in the polluted canal water, using goods wagons idling in the railway sidings as improvised changing huts. A colourful underground community also operated illegal gambling dens. The last regular canal users were the sugar boats from the Sankey sugar works at Newton-le-Willows, before the canal was closed in 1963.

In the 1970s Spike Island was transformed into the green open space and haven for wildlife it is today. Opened by the Queen in 1977, it is now a mixture of grassland and semi-mature woodland planted with native species of oak and beech (plus some birch).

Off Spike Island, West Bank's shrimp fishing fleet was moored. One shrimper still puts out from opposite the Visitors' Centre (tel. 051 420 3707), where a miscellany of colourful craft line the wharf. Anglers even catch the occasional eel.

In woodland glades, flowers of snowdrop, primrose and bluebell are followed by foxglove, teasel and campion. Tansy, ox-eye daisy, toadflax (bastard and common), cranesbill and orange hawkweed thrive in more open meadowland, where butterflies flit - the common speckled wood and meadow brown, plus an occasional comma and clouded yellow.

A PLACE TO VISIT

Catalyst Museum
Overlooking Spike Island and created in the cradle of the United Kingdom's Chemical Industry, is the world's first chemical museum. Appropriately, it is housed in Hutchinson's Works which, after his death, were used as offices and laboratories by Gossage.

Open every day except Monday, here the Chemical Industry is explored through hands-on exhibits and demonstrations. The external glass lift provides a panoramic view as does the observation gallery, 100 feet above ground level. (Telephone: 051 420 1121)

Birds of the Estuary
Widnes Warth was the original name for this area and Widnes Warth Marsh still fronts the River Mersey between Spike Island and Fiddler's Ferry, a salt marsh where sea aster and scurvy grass thrive, and where hen harrier and short-eared owl hunt in Winter. The estuary is also the winter home of pintail, teal and wigeon, and waders such as shelduck and redshank feed on the mudflats.

Vapour from the cooling towers of Fiddler's Ferry rises into a cloudless sky.

Fiddler's Ferry

Along the towpath stands Fiddler's Ferry Power Station. The first part of its name originated from the first owner of the nearby Manor of Penketh - Adam de Violeur (Violeur meaning a violin player or fiddler).

Since the 12th century, a ferry is said to have crossed the River Mersey from here. The *Ferry Inn*, which dates back to 1762, was built on its site and now also lends its name to the power station. Reputedly, the inn is haunted by Charlie, an ancient ferryman who smoked Jamaican tobacco.

Built during the 1960s, this massive power station has now been taken over by *PowerGen*. It can produce enough electricity to meet the needs of two million people - sufficent to satisfy the demands of all those living in Liverpool and Manchester at peak power time.

Operating at full capacity the station burns 19,000 tonnes of coal a day and 18 loads arrive daily by train. Much of the ash waste is sold to the building trade, to be used for making breezeblocks.

The cooling process uses 263 million litres of water an hour, much of which comes from the River Mersey and is then either recycled back into the river, or goes into the huge lagoons nearby. The cooling towers dominate the skyline and, at a height of 655 feet, the chimney is probably the tallest manmade structure in Cheshire.

In the 1980s one of the canal's twin locks here was restored to provide access from canal to river, and today there is sheltered mooring and a boatyard. Opened in 1856, the train station was closed in 1950 but the station master's house remains and the goods' yard provides a car park.

TOURIST INFORMATION CENTRES

Warrington   21 Rylands Street, Warrington, WA1 1EJ
Tel: 0925 636501

Runcorn   57-61 Church Street, Runcorn, WA7 1LG
Tel: 0928 569656, 576776

Widnes   Municipal Buildings, Kingsway, Widnes, WA8 7QF
Tel: 051 424 2061 (ext. 4132)

ORGANISATIONS

The Mersey Valley Partnership: The Coach House, Norton Priory, Tudor Road, Manor Park, Runcorn, Cheshire, WA7 1SX *Tel:* 0928 573346

Mid-Cheshire Footpath Society: Ernie Vickers, 8 Mansefield Road, Kingsley, Cheshire, WA6 8BZ. *Tel:* 0928 788019

Cheshire Wildlife Trust: Grebe House, Reaseheath, Nantwich, CW5 6DA. *Tel:* 0270 610180

CPRE: Cheshire Branch, Victoria Buildings, Middlewich, Cheshire, CW10 9AT. *Tel:* 0606 835046

The Mersey Forest: Risley Moss, Ordnance Avenue, Birchwood, Warrington, WA3 6QX. *Tel:* 0925 816217

Woodland Trust: Cheshire's Local Officer: Simon Mageean, Lilac Cottage, Fir Tree Lane, Littleton, Chester, CH3 7DH. *Tel:* 0244 336868

ABOUT THE AUTHOR

Jen Darling has lived in Cheshire for the past 26 years. Married with four children, all now adult, she left teaching in 1986 and has since written several successful books about the county. She is a life member of the Mid-Cheshire Footpath Society and walks with them whenever time allows.

West Cheshire Walks, *Portrait of Warrington* and *Pub Walks in Cheshire* were all published at the turn of the decade. *Twelve Town Trails in Cheshire* followed, gleaned from articles written for *Cheshire Life*. Jen has also produced crossword books for children, offers a desk top publishing service and has worked as a sub-editor on the local paper.

Other interests include playing tennis in Stockton Heath, bell ringing at St. Matthew's, Stretton, attending a weekly french conversation class at Lymm, and editing Warrington's Talking Newspaper for the Blind. She also gardens and occasionally cycles with her husband.

OTHER TITLES

West Cheshire Walks *(Sigma)*   £5.95
Forty circular walks of varying lengths, from
Warrington to Whitchurch, Wilmslow to Wirral.

Portrait of Warrington *(Sigma)*   £6.95
Lavishly illustrated, it moves from Ice Age to New Town.

Warrington Town Trail *(Alfresco)*   95p
A fascinating hour's walk takes you back in time.

Pub Walks in Cheshire *(Sigma)*   £6.95
First in this popular series. Thirty circular walks from historic
inns serving Real Ale and appetising food.

Twelve Town Trails in Cheshire *(Alfresco)*   £4.25
Short walks into the countryside from Cheshire and Wirral's
picturesque townships.

Crosswords for Children - Book 1 *(Alfresco)*   95p
Crosswords for Children - Book 2 *(Alfresco)*   95p
Ideal as stocking fillers, on car journeys, on holiday, in school ...
(A special discount will be given for orders of 10 or more.)

Family Cycling in North Cheshire by Lyn Goodkin *(Alfresco)* £6.95
Twelve circular cycle rides with lots of interest along the way.

Available from all good bookshops or contact:
Alfresco Books: 7 Pineways, Appleton, Warrington, WA4 5EJ
Tel: 0925 267503

STUCK FOR WORDS
Desk Top Publishing Service
writing - editing - proof reading
all pre-press work to camera ready output
Tel: 0925 267503